ARCTIC REGION AND ANTARCTICA ISSUES AND RESEARCH SERIES

ARCTIC NATURAL RESOURCES

ARCTIC REGION AND ANTARCTICA ISSUES AND RESEARCH

Arctic National Wildlife Refuge
Cogwell, Mathew T. (Editor)
2009. ISBN: 1-59033-327-6

The Arctic Observing Network
Thomas R. Calahan
2009. ISBN: 978-1-60692-847-9

The Pacific and Arctic Oceans: New Oceanographic Research
Kallen B. Tewles (Editor)
2009. ISBN: 978-1-60692-010-7

The Pacific and Arctic Oceans: New Oceanographic Research
Kallen B. Tewles (Editor)
2009. ISBN: 978-1-60876-749-6 (Online Book)

Arctic Natural Resources
Brian D. Raney
2009. ISBN: 978-1-60692-131-9

ARCTIC REGION AND ANTARCTICA ISSUES AND RESEARCH SERIES

ARCTIC NATURAL RESOURCES

BRIAN D. RANEY
EDITOR

Nova Science Publishers, Inc.
New York

For permission to use material from this book please contact us:
Telephone 631-231-7269; Fax 631-231-8175
Web Site: http://www.novapublishers.com

NOTICE TO THE READER

The Publisher has taken reasonable care in the preparation of this book, but makes no expressed or implied warranty of any kind and assumes no responsibility for any errors or omissions. No liability is assumed for incidental or consequential damages in connection with or arising out of information contained in this book. The Publisher shall not be liable for any special, consequential, or exemplary damages resulting, in whole or in part, from the readers' use of, or reliance upon, this material. Any parts of this book based on government reports are so indicated and copyright is claimed for those parts to the extent applicable to compilations of such works.

Independent verification should be sought for any data, advice or recommendations contained in this book. In addition, no responsibility is assumed by the publisher for any injury and/or damage to persons or property arising from any methods, products, instructions, ideas or otherwise contained in this publication.

This publication is designed to provide accurate and authoritative information with regard to the subject matter covered herein. It is sold with the clear understanding that the Publisher is not engaged in rendering legal or any other professional services. If legal or any other expert assistance is required, the services of a competent person should be sought. FROM A DECLARATION OF PARTICIPANTS JOINTLY ADOPTED BY A COMMITTEE OF THE AMERICAN BAR ASSOCIATION AND A COMMITTEE OF PUBLISHERS.

LIBRARY OF CONGRESS CATALOGING-IN-PUBLICATION DATA

Arctic natural resources / editor, Brian D. Raney.
   p. cm.
 Includes index.
 ISBN 978-1-60692-131-9 (softcover)
 1. Natural resources--Arctic Regions. I. Raney, Brian D.
 HC733.5.A74 2009
 333.70911'3--dc22   2009028444

Published by Nova Science Publishers, Inc. + New York

CONTENTS

PREFACE

A major part of the energy debate is whether to approve energy development in the Arctic National Wildlife Refuge (ANWR) in northeastern Alaska, and if so, under what conditions, or whether to continue to prohibit development to protect the area's biological resources. ANWR is rich in fauna, flora and commercial oil potential. Its development has been debated for over 40 years, but increasing gasoline and natural gas prices, terrorist attacks and infrastructure damage from hurricanes have intensified the debate. Current law forbids energy leasing in ANWR. This book provides a summary of legislative attempts to address the issues of energy development and preservation in the Refuge. ANWR consists of 19 million acres in northeast Alaska. The Refuge and especially the coastal plain, is home to a wide variety of plants and animals. The presence of caribou, polar bears, grizzly bears, wolves and migratory birds, and many other species in a nearly undisturbed state has led some to call the area "America's Serengeti." This book covers, first, the economic and geological factors that have triggered new interest in development, followed by the philosophical, biological and environmental quality factors that have triggered opposition to it.

Chapter 1 - A major part of the energy debate is whether to approve energy development in the Arctic National Wildlife Refuge (ANWR) in northeastern Alaska, and if so, under what conditions, or whether to continue to prohibit development to protect the area's biological resources. ANWR is rich in fauna, flora, and commercial oil potential. Its development has been debated for over 40 years, but increases in gasoline and natural gas prices, terrorist attacks, and infrastructure damage from hurricanes have intensified the debate. Current law forbids energy leasing in ANWR.

Chapter 2 - Congress is again considering whether to permit drilling for oil and gas on the coastal plain of the Arctic National Wildlife Refuge (ANWR), Alaska, or to maintain the current statutory prohibition on oil and gas development in the Refuge. The 109th Congress has considered the issue in authorizing bills, budget reconciliation bills, and an appropriation bill, but legislation opening the Refuge has not yet passed both chambers. Several measures would have limited the surface area that could be covered by certain oil production and support facilities to 2,000 acres of the 1.5 million acres of the Coastal Plain. These provisions raise several issues: they may not apply to some or all of the nearly 100,000 acres held by Native Americans in the Refuge that could be developed if the federal lands are opened to oil and gas development; and exactly what facilities would be subject to the limitation is not clear, although the limitation could constrain development if oil and gas discoveries are widespread. This chapter discusses both legal and technical aspects of the 2,000-acre limit.

Chapter 3 – This Open-File report contains illustrative materials, in the form of PowerPoint slides, used for an oral presentation given at the Fourth U.S. Geological Survey Workshop on Reserve Growth of petroleum resources held on March 10-11, 2008. The presentation focused on engineering and economic aspects of the Circum-Arctic Oil and Gas Resource Appraisal (CARA) project, with a special emphasis on the costs related to the development of hypothetical oil and gas fields of different sizes and reservoir characteristics in the North Danmarkshavn Basin off the northeast coast of Greenland.

The individual PowerPoint slides highlight the topics being addressed in an abbreviated format; they are discussed below, and are amplified with additional text as appropriate. Also included in this report are the summary results of a typical "run" to generate the necessary capital and operating costs for the development of an offshore oil field off the northeast coast of Greenland; the data are displayed in MS Excel format generated using Questor software (IHS Energy, Inc.).

U.S. Geological Survey (USGS) acknowledges that this report includes data supplied by IHS Energy, Inc.; Copyright (2008) all rights reserved. IHS Energy has granted USGS the permission to publish this report.

Chapter 4 - In 2007, the U.S. Geological Survey (USGS) completed an assessment of potential undiscovered, technically recoverable (assuming the absence of sea ice) crude oil, natural gas, and natural gas liquids (collectively referred to as petroleum) resources in the Yenisey-Khatanga Basin, Lena-Anabar Basin, Lena-Vilyui Basin (northern part), and the Zyryanka Basin

Provinces of the Russian Federation. As with other areas and basins assessed in the USGS Circum-Arctic Oil and Gas Resource Appraisal (CARA) program, this area shares important characteristics with many Arctic basins, including sparse data, significant petroleum-resource potential, geologic uncertainty, and technical barriers that impede exploration and development. As defined for CARA, the Yenisey-Khatanga Basin Province includes approximately 391,000 km^2; the Lena-Anabar Basin Province, approximately 125,000 km^2; the northern Priverkhoyansk part of the Lena-Vilyuy Basin Province, approximately 55,000 km^2, and the Zyryanka Basin Province, approximately 56,000 km^2.

Chapter 5 - In 2007, the U.S. Geological Survey (USGS) completed an assessment of potential undiscovered, technically recoverable (assuming the absence of sea ice) crude oil, natural gas, and natural gas liquids (collectively referred to as petroleum) resources in the Laptev Sea Shelf Province of the Russian Federation. As with other areas assessed in the USGS Circum-Arctic Oil and Gas Resource Appraisal (CARA), this area shares important characteristics with many Arctic basins, including sparse data, significant petroleum-resource potential, geologic uncertainty, and technical barriers that impede exploration and development. As defined for CARA, the province includes an area of approximately 500,000 km^2, most of which underlies less than 500 m of water offshore of northern Russia between long. 110° and 150° E. and between lat. 70° and 80° N.

Chapter 6 - In 2007 the U.S. Geological Survey (USGS) completed an assessment of the potential for undiscovered, technically recoverable (assuming the absence of sea ice) oil and gas resources in the East Greenland Rift Basins Province. Northeast Greenland has been selected as the prototype for the new U.S. Geological Survey Circum-Arctic Resource Appraisal (CARA) because the area shares important characteristics with many arctic basins, including sparse data, significant resource potential, great geological uncertainty, and significant technical barriers to exploration and development. This study, which supersedes a previous USGS assessment of the same area completed in 2000, was necessary because of new information made available through collaboration with the Geological Survey of Denmark and Greenland (GEUS), which significantly changes the geological understanding of the area.

As defined for CARA, the province includes an area of approximately 500,000 square kilometers, most of which underlies less than 500 meters of water offshore east of Greenland between 70° and 82° North.

Chapter 7 - The U.S. Geological Survey (USGS) recently assessed the undiscovered oil and gas potential of the West Greenland— East Canada

Province as part of the USGS Circum-Arctic Oil and Gas Resource Appraisal effort. The West Greenland—East Canada Province is essentially the offshore area between west Greenland and east Canada and includes Baffin Bay, Davis Strait, Lancaster Sound, and Nares Strait west of and including Kane Basin. The tectonic evolution of the West Greenland—East Canada Province led to the formation of several major structural domains that are the geologic basis for the five assessment units (AU) defined in this study. The five AUs encompass the entire province Each AU was assessed in its entirety for undiscovered, technically recoverable (assuming absence of sea ice) oil and gas resources, but the assessment results reported here are only for those portions of each AU that are north of the Arctic Circle, as that latitude defines the area of the Circum-Arctic oil and gas assessment.

In: Arctic Natural Resources
Editor: Brian D. Raney

ISBN: 978-1-60692-131-9
© 2009 Nova Science Publishers, Inc.

Chapter 1

ARCTIC NATIONAL WILDLIFE REFUGE (ANWR): LEGISLATIVE ACTIONS THROUGH THE 109TH CONGRESS

Anne Gillis[1], M. Lynne Corn, Bernard A. Gelb[2] and Pamela Baldwin[3]

SUMMARY

A major part of the energy debate is whether to approve energy development in the Arctic National Wildlife Refuge (ANWR) in northeastern Alaska, and if so, under what conditions, or whether to continue to prohibit development to protect the area's biological resources. ANWR is rich in fauna, flora, and commercial oil potential. Its development has been debated for over 40 years, but increases in gasoline and natural gas prices, terrorist attacks, and infrastructure damage from hurricanes have intensified the debate. Current law forbids energy leasing in ANWR.

This report is intended to provide a summary of legislative attempts to address issues of energy development and preservation in the Refuge from the 95th Congress through the 109th Congress, with emphasis on the 107th through

---

[1] Anne Gillis, Information Research Specialist, Knowledge Services Group
[2] M. Lynne Corn and Bernard A. Gelb, Specialist in Natural Resources and, Specialist in Industry Economics, Resources, Science, and Industry Division
[3] Pamela Baldwin, Consultant, American Law Division

109th Congresses. This history has been cited by many, in and out of Congress, as background for issues that may be raised in the 110th Congress. The report contains little analysis of the substance of this issue, which is covered in other CRS reports. See CRS Report RL33872, *Arctic National Wildlife Refuge (ANWR): New Directions in the 110th Congress*, for information on actions in the 110th Congress relative to ANWR.

The ANWR debate took two basic legislative routes in the 109th Congress: (1) budget resolutions and reconciliation bills (S.Con.Res. 18, H.Con.Res. 95, S. 1932, H.R. 4241, S.Con.Res. 83, and H.Con.Res. 376), which cannot be filibustered; and (2) other bills (H.R. 6, an omnibus energy bill; H.R. 2863, Defense appropriations; and H.R. 5429, a bill in the second session to open the Refuge to development), which are subject to filibusters. In none of these measures did Congress reach agreement to allow development.

In the first session of the 109th Congress, development advocates added ANWR development to the conference report for the Defense appropriations bill (H.R. 2863). The House passed the conference report with the ANWR provision, but the ANWR title was removed from the bill (P.L. 109-148) after failure of a cloture motion in the Senate.

In the second session, on March 16, 2006, the Senate passed S.Con.Res. 83, the FY2007 budget resolution. Its sole reconciliation instruction was to the Senate Committee on Energy and Natural Resources, and it assumed revenues from leasing in ANWR. On May 25, 2006, the House passed the American-Made Energy and Good Jobs Act (H.R. 5429), which would have opened ANWR to development.

BACKGROUND AND ANALYSIS

The Arctic National Wildlife Refuge (ANWR) consists of 19 million acres in northeast Alaska. It is administered by the Fish and Wildlife Service (FWS) in the Department of the Interior (DOI). Its 1.5 million acre coastal plain on the North Slope of the Brooks Range is currently viewed as one of the most likely undeveloped U.S. onshore oil and gas prospects. According to the U.S. Geological Survey, there is even a small chance that taken together, the fields on this federal land could hold as much economically recoverable oil as the giant field at Prudhoe Bay, found in 1967 on the coastal plain west of ANWR. That state-owned portion of the coastal plain is now estimated to have held 11 billion to 13 billion barrels of oil.

The Refuge, and especially the coastal plain, is home to a wide variety of plants and animals. The presence of caribou, polar bears, grizzly bears, wolves, migratory birds, and many other species in a nearly undisturbed state has led some to call the area "America's Serengeti." The Refuge and two neighboring parks in Canada have been proposed for an international park, and several species found in the area (including polar bears, caribou, migratory birds, and whales) are protected by international treaties or agreements. The analysis below covers, first, the economic and geological factors that have triggered new interest in development, followed by the philosophical, biological, and environmental quality factors that have triggered opposition to it. That analysis is followed by a history of congressional actions on this issue, with a focus on those in the 107th Congress through the 109th Congress. See Tables 1 and 2 for votes in the House and Senate from the 96th Congress through the 109th Congress.

The conflict between high oil potential and nearly pristine nature creates a dilemma: should Congress open the area for oil and gas development, or should the area's ecosystem be given permanent protection from development? What factors should determine whether to open the area? If the area is opened, how can damages be avoided, minimized, or mitigated? To what extent should Congress legislate special management of the area (if it is developed), and to what extent should federal agencies be allowed to manage the area under existing law? If Congress takes no action, the Refuge remains closed to energy development.

Table 1. Votes in the House of Representatives on Energy Development Within the Arctic National Wildlife Refuge

Congress	Date	Voice/ Roll Call	Brief Description
95th			no floor votes
96th	5/16/79	#152	Udall-Anderson substitute for H.R. 39 adopted by House (268-157); included provisions designating all of ANWR as wilderness.
	5/16/79	#153	H.R 39 passed House (360-65).
	11/12/80	voice (unanimous)	Senate version (leaving 1002 area development issue to a future Congress) of H.R. 39 passed House.
97th			no floor votes
98th			no floor votes

Table 1. (Continued)

Congress	Date	Voice/ Roll Call	Brief Description
99th			no floor votes
100th			no floor votes
101st			no floor votes
102nd			no floor votes
103rd			no floor votes
104th	11/17/95	#812	House agreed (237-189) to conference report on H.R. 2491 (H.Rept. 104-350), FY1996 budget reconciliation (a large bill that included 1002 area development pro-visions; see text).
105th			no floor votes
106th			no floor votes
107th	8/1/01	#316	House passed Sununu amendment to H.R. 4 to limit specified surface development of 1002 area to a total of 2,000 acres (228-201).
	8/1/01	#317	House rejected Markey-Johnson (CT) amendment to H.R. 4 to strike 1002 area development title (206-223).
	8/2/01	#320	H.R. 4, an omnibus energy bill, passed House (240-189). Title V of Division F contained 1002 area development provisions.
108th	4/10/03	#134	House passed Wilson (NM) amendment to H.R. 6 to limit certain features of 1002 area development to a total of 2,000 acres (226-202).
	4/10/03	#135	House rejected Markey-Johnson (CT) amendment to H.R. 6 to strike 1002 area development title (197-228).
	4/11/03	#145	House passed H.R. 6, a comprehensive energy bill (247-175); Division C, Title IV would have opened the 1002 area to energy development.
109th	3/17/05	#88	House adopted (218-214) the concurrent budget resolution, H.Con.Res. 95, which included spending targets that would be difficult to achieve unless ANWR development legislation was passed.
	4/20/05	#122	House rejected (200-231) Markey amendment to strike the ANWR provision in its omnibus energy bill (H.R. 6) allowing leases for exploration, development, and production in ANWR.

Table 1. (Continued)

Congress	Date	Voice/ Roll Call	Brief Description
	4/21/05	#132	House passed an omnibus energy bill (H.R. 6) with an ANWR development title (249-183).
	4/28/05	#149	House adopted (214-211) the conference report on the concurrent budget resolution, H.Con.Res. 95.
	12/18/05	#669	House adopted (308-106) the conference report on the Defense appropriations bill (H.R. 2863), which would have allowed oil and gas leasing in ANWR.
	12/22/05	voice	House passed S.Con.Res. 74, which corrected the enrollment of H.R. 2863, removing the ANWR development provision.
	5/25/06	#209	House passed H.R. 5429 to open ANWR to development (225-201).

Table 2. Votes in the Senate on Energy Development within the Arctic National Wildlife Refuge

Congress	Date	Voice/ Roll Call	Brief Description
95th			no floor votes
96th	7/22-23/80	#304	Motion to table Tsongas amendment (including a title to designate all of ANWR as wilderness) to H.R. 39 defeated (33-64).
	8/18/80	#354	Senate adopted cloture motion on H.R. 39 (63-25).
	8/19/80	#359	Senate passed Tsongas-Roth-Jackson-Hatfield substitute to H.R. 39 (78-14); this bill is current law, and leaves decision about any 1002 area development for a future Congress.
97th			no floor votes
98th			no floor votes
99th			no floor votes
100th			no floor votes
101st			no floor votes
102nd	11/1/91	#242	Cloture motion on S. 1220 failed; one title would have opened 1002 area to development (50-44).

Table 2. (Continued)

Congress	Date	Voice/ Roll Call	Brief Description
103rd			no floor votes
104th	5/24/95	#190	Senate voted to table Roth amendment to strip 1002 area revenue assumptions from S.Con. Res. 13 (56-44).
	10/27/95	#525	Senate voted to table Baucus amendment to strip 1002 area development provisions in H.R. 2491 (51-48).
105th			no floor votes
106th	4/6/00	#58	Senate voted to table Roth amendment to strip 1002 area revenue assumptions from the FY20-01 budget resolution (S.Con.Res. 101) (51-49).
107th	12/3/01	#344	Lott-Murkowski-Brownback amendment to Daschle amendment to H.R. 10 included 1002 area development title in H.R. 4, as passed by the House. A cloture motion on the amend-ment failed (1-94).
	4/18/02	#71	Senate failed to invoke cloture on Murkowski amendment to S. 517, an omnibus energy bill. ANWR language of the amendment was similar to that in the House-passed version of H.R. 4 (46-54).
108th	3/19/03	#59	Senate passed Boxer amendment to delete cer-tain revenue assumptions from S.Con.Res. 23, the FY2004 budget resolution; floor debate in-dicated that the amendment was clearly seen as a vote on developing the 1002 area (52-48).
109th	3/16/05	#52	Senate voted to reject Cantwell amendment to strike revenue assumptions from its FY2006 budget resolution (S.Con.Res. 18) that would have given procedural protection to legislation authorizing oil drilling in part of ANWR (49-51).
	11/3/05	#288	Senate voted to reject Cantwell amendment to its FY2006 budget reconciliation bill (S.1932) that would have deleted the provision establi-shing an oil and gas leasing program in ANWR (48-51).
	12/21/05	#364	Senate failed to invoke cloture on the conference report on the FY2006 Defense appropriations bill (H.R. 2863), which included provisions to open ANWR to development (56-44).

Congress	Date	Voice /Roll Call	Brief Description
	12/21/05	#365	Senate adopted a concurrent resolution (S.Con. Res. 74) that instructed the Clerk of the House to strike provisions from the conference report to H.R. 2863 that would have allowed oil drilling in ANWR (48-45).
	3/16/06	#74	Senate passed the FY2007 budget resolution (S.Con.Res. 83) with a reconciliation instruction (§201) directing the Committee on Energy and Natural Resources to reduce budget authority by an amount equal to assumed revenues from development in ANWR (51-49).

Legislative History of the Refuge, 1957-2000

The Early Years

The energy and biological resources of northern Alaska have raised controversy for decades, from legislation in the 1970s, to a 1989 oil spill, to more recent efforts to use ANWR resources to address energy needs or to help balance the federal budget. In November 1957, DOI announced plans to withdraw lands in northeastern Alaska to create an "Arctic National Wildlife Range." The first group actually to propose to Congress that the area become a national wildlife range, in recognition of the many game species found in the area, was the Tanana Valley (Alaska) Sportsmen's Association in 1959. On December 6, 1960, after statehood, the Secretary of the Interior issued Public Land Order 2214 reserving the 9.5 millionacre area as the Arctic National Wildlife Range.

The 1970s

In 1971, Congress enacted the Alaska Native Claims Settlement Act (ANCSA, P.L. 92-203, 85 Stat. 688) to resolve all Native aboriginal land claims against the United States. ANCSA provided for monetary payments and also created Village Corporations that received the surface estate to approximately 22 million acres of lands in Alaska. Village selection rights included the right to choose the surface estate (surface rights, as opposed to rights to exploit any energy or minerals beneath the surface) in a certain amount of lands within the National Wildlife Refuge System. Under §22(g) of ANCSA, the chosen lands were to remain subject to the laws and regulations governing use and development of the particular refuge. Kaktovik Inupiat Corporation (KIC, the local Native corporation created under ANCSA, and headquartered within ANWR) received rights to three townships along the coast of ANWR. ANCSA also created Regional Corporations, which could select subsurface rights to some lands and full title to others. Subsurface rights in national wildlife refuges were not available, but in-lieu selections to substitute for such lands were provided.

The 1980s

In 1980, Congress enacted the Alaska National Interest Lands Conservation Act (ANILCA, P.L. 96-487, 94 Stat. 2371), which included several sections about ANWR. The Arctic Range was renamed the Arctic National Wildlife Refuge, and was expanded, mostly southward and westward, to include an additional 9.2 million acres.[2] Section 702(3) of ANILCA designated much of the original range as a wilderness area, but did not include the coastal plain.[3] ANILCA defined the *Coastal Plain* as the lands on a specified map — language that was interpreted as excluding most Native lands, even though these lands are *geographically* part of the coastal plain.[4] Section 1002 of ANILCA directed that a study of the Coastal Plain (which therefore is often referred to as the *1002 area*) and its resources be completed within five years and nine months of enactment. The resulting 1987 report was called the *1002 report* or the Final Legislative Environmental Impact Statement (FLEIS).

Section 1003 of ANILCA prohibited oil and gas development in the entire Refuge, or "leasing or other development leading to production of oil and gas from the range" unless authorized by an act of Congress.[5]

From 1990 to 2000

In recent years, there have been various attempts to authorize opening ANWR to energy development. In the 104th Congress, the FY1996 budget reconciliation bill (H.R. 2491, §§5312-5344) would have opened the 1002 area to energy development, but the measure was vetoed, as many observers had expected. President Clinton cited the ANWR sections as one of his reasons for the veto.

While bills were introduced, the 105th Congress did not debate the ANWR issue. In the 106th Congress, bills to designate the 1002 area of the Refuge as wilderness and others to open the Refuge to energy development were introduced. Revenue assumptions about ANWR were included in the FY2001 budget resolution (S.Con.Res. 101) reported by the Senate Budget Committee on March 31, 2000. An amendment to remove this language was tabled. However, conferees rejected the language. The conference report on H.Con.Res. 290 did not contain this assumption, and the report was passed by both chambers on April 13. S. 2557 was introduced May 16, 2000; it included a title to open the Refuge to development. Hearings were held on the bill, but a motion to proceed to consideration of the bill on the Senate floor did not pass.

Only three recorded votes relating directly to ANWR development occurred from the 101st through 106th Congresses. All were in the Senate:

- In the 104th Congress, on May 24 1995, a motion to table an amendment that would have stripped ANWR development titles from the Senate version of H.R. 2491 passed (Roll Call #190). (See above.)
- In the same Congress, on October 27, 1995, another motion to table a similar amendment to H.R. 2491 also passed (Roll Call #525).
- In the 106th Congress, the vote to table an amendment to strip ANWR revenue assumptions from the budget resolution (S.Con.Res. 101; see above) was passed (April 6, 2000, Roll Call #58).

Legislative History of the Refuge, 2001-2002

H.R. 4, an omnibus energy bill containing ANWR development provisions, passed the House on August 2, 2001 (yeas 240, nays 189; Roll Call #320). Title V of Division F was the text of H.R. 2436 (H.Rept. 107-160, Part I). The measure would have opened ANWR to exploration and development. The previous day, an amendment by then Representative Sununu to limit specified surface development to a total of 2,000 acres was passed (yeas 228, nays 201; Roll Call #316). Representatives Markey and Johnson (CT) offered an amendment to strike the title; this was defeated (yeas 206, nays 223; Roll

Call #317). The House appointed conferees on June 12, 2002. (See below for action after Senate passage of H.R. 4.)

In the first session, Senator Lott (on behalf of himself and Senators Murkowski and Brownback) offered an amendment (S.Amdt. 2171) to an amendment on pension reform (S.Amdt. 2170) to H.R. 10, a bill also on pension reform. Their amendment included, among other energy provisions, the ANWR development title in H.R. 4, as passed by the House. Their amendment also included provisions prohibiting cloning of human tissue. A cloture motion was filed on the Lott amendment, and the Senate failed to invoke cloture (yeas 1, nays 94; Roll Call #344) on December 3, 2001. Instead, the Senate voted the same day in favor of invoking cloture on the underlying amendment (S.Amdt. 2170), (yeas 81, nays 15; Roll Call #345). Because cloture was invoked on the underlying amendment, Senate rules required that subsequent and pending amendments to it be germane. The Senate's presiding officer subsequently sustained a point of order against the Lott amendment, which was still pending, on the grounds that it was not germane to the underlying amendment on pension reform, and thus the amendment fell.

The next vehicle for Senate floor consideration was S. 517, which concerned energy technology development. On February 15, 2002, Senator Daschle offered an amendment (S.Amdt. 2917), an omnibus energy bill. It did not contain provisions to develop the Refuge, but two amendments (S.Amdt. 3132 and S.Amdt. 3133) to do so were offered by Senators Murkowski and Stevens, respectively, on April 16. The language of the two amendments was, in most sections, identical to that of H.R. 4 (Division F, Title V). Key differences included a requirement for a presidential determination before development could proceed, an exception to the oil export prohibition for Israel, and a number of changes in allocation of any development revenues, as well as allowing some of those revenues to be spent without further appropriation. On April 18, the Senate essentially voted to prevent drilling for oil and gas in the Refuge. The defeat came on a vote of 46 yeas to 54 nays (Roll Call #71) on a cloture motion to block a threatened filibuster on Senator Murkowski's amendment to S. 517, which would have ended debate and moved the chamber to a direct vote on the ANWR issue.

Lacking a provision to develop ANWR, the text of S. 517, as amended, was substituted for the text of the House-passed H.R. 4, and passed the Senate (yeas 88, nays 11; Roll Call #94) on April 25, 2002. Conferees attempted to iron out the substantial differences between the two versions in the time remaining in the second session. The conference committee chairman,

Representative Tauzin, indicated that the ANWR issue, as one of the most controversial parts of the bill, would be considered toward the end of the conference, after less controversial provisions. Press reports at the time indicated that conferees were likely to drop provisions to develop the Refuge. Interior Secretary Norton stated that she would recommend veto of a bill lacking ANWR development provisions.[6] In the end, no conference agreement was reached, and H.R. 4 died at the end of the 107th Congress.

Finally, H.R. 770 and S. 411 would have designated the 1002 area as wilderness, but no action was taken on either bill.

Legislative History of the Refuge, 2003-2004

Work began on FY2003 Interior appropriations in the 107th Congress but was not completed until the 108th Congress. In the 107th Congress, for the FY2003 Interior appropriations bill, the House Committee on Appropriations had agreed to report language on the Bureau of Land Management (BLM) energy and minerals program in general, and stated that no funds were included in the FY2003 funding bill "for activity related to potential energy development within [ANWR]" (H.Rept. 107-564, H.R. 5093). But §1003 of ANILCA prohibited "development leading to production of oil and gas" unless authorized by Congress. Thus, the committee's report language was viewed by some as barring the use of funds for pre-leasing studies and other preliminary work related to oil and gas drilling in ANWR. The report of the Senate Committee on Appropriations did not contain this prohibition. A series of continuing resolutions provided funding for DOI into the 108th Congress.

Conferees on the FY2003 Consolidated Appropriations Resolution (P.L. 108-7) included language in the joint explanatory statement stating that they "do not concur with the House proposal concerning funding for the [BLM] energy and minerals program." This change from the House report language was interpreted by some as potentially making available funds for preliminary work for development in ANWR. However, as noted, the prohibition contained in ANILCA remains in effect, so the ability to use money in the bill for particular pre-leasing activities was not clear.

FY2004 Reconciliation

During the 108th Congress, development proponents sought to move ANWR legislation through the FY2004 budget reconciliation process to avoid a possible Senate filibuster later in the session.[7] The House agreed to the FY2004 budget resolution (H.Con.Res. 95) on March 21 (yeas 215, nays 212; Roll Call #82). The resolution contained reconciliation instructions to the House Resources Committee for reductions, but did not specify the expected source of the savings. If the House language had been adopted, ANWR development language might have been considered as part of a reconciliation measure to achieve the savings. S.Con.Res. 23, as reported by the Senate Budget Committee, stated:

> The Senate Committee on Energy and Natural Resources shall report a reconciliation bill not later than May 1, 2003, that consists of changes in laws within its jurisdiction sufficient to decrease the total level of outlays by $2,150,000,000 for the period of fiscal years 2004 through 2013.

To meet this directive, the committee would very likely have reported legislation to open ANWR to development. On March 19, 2003, Senator Boxer offered S.Amdt. 272 to delete this provision. Floor debate indicated that the Boxer amendment was clearly seen as a vote on developing ANWR. The amendment passed (yeas 52, nays 48; Roll Call #59.) The amended Senate version of the resolution was ultimately accepted by both House and Senate. As a result, while the Committee on Energy and Natural Resources could still report legislation to authorize opening the Refuge, such legislation would not have been eligible for inclusion in a reconciliation bill. Without the procedural protections associated with reconciliation, a filibuster could have been used to prevent a vote on an authorization bill.[8] In the end, the conferees on the budget resolution included no instructions to the House Resources and Senate Energy and Natural Resources Committees.

Comprehensive Energy Legislation

The House passed H.R. 6, a comprehensive energy bill, on April 11, 2003. Division C, Title IV would have opened the 1002 area to energy development. On April 10, the House had passed the Wilson (NM) amendment to H.R. 6 to limit certain features of development to a total of 2,000 acres (yeas 226, nays

202; Roll Call #134), without restricting the total number of acres that could be leased. As in the 107th Congress, Representatives Markey and Johnson (CT) offered an amendment to strike the title; this was defeated (yeas 197, nays 228; Roll Call #135). H.R. 4514 was identical to the ANWR title of the House version of H.R. 6 except in one provision on revenue disposition. (See "Major Legislative Issues," below.) In addition, one bill (H.R. 39) was introduced to open the 1002 area to development, and two bills (H.R. 770 and S. 543) were introduced to designate the 1002 area as wilderness.

The initial version of the Senate energy bill (S. 14) had no provision to open the Refuge, and Chairman Domenici stated that he did not plan to include one. After many weeks of debate in the Senate, as prospects of passage seemed to be dimming, Senators agreed to drop the bill they had been debating and to go back to the bill passed in the Democratic-controlled Senate of the 107th Congress. On July 31, 2003, they substituted the language of that bill for that of the House-passed H.R. 6. There was widespread agreement that the unusual procedure was a means of getting the bill to conference. Members, including Chairman Domenici, indicated at the time their expectation that the bill that emerged from conference would likely be markedly different from the bill that had just been passed by the Senate. One of the key differences between the two bills was the presence of ANWR development language in the House version, and its absence in the Senate version. Conference Chairman Domenici included the House title on ANWR in his working draft, but in the end, the conference committee deleted ANWR development features in the conference report (H.Rept. 108-375); the conference report was agreed to by the House on November 18, 2003 (yeas 246, nays 180; Roll Call #630); the Senate considered the measure, but a cloture vote failed (57 yeas, 40 nays; Roll Call # 456) on November 21, 2003.

The Senate focused in the second session on a reduced energy bill (S. 2095) that might then go to a second conference with the House; like its version of H.R. 6, this new bill did not contain ANWR development provisions. In any event, no scenario for energy legislation that was discussed publicly included provisions that would have opened the Refuge to development. However, the President's proposed FY2005 budget assumed legislation would be passed that would open the Refuge and would therefore produce revenues. This proposal would have assisted efforts to assume ANWR revenues in a budget resolution, and therefore aided its inclusion in a reconciliation package, as was attempted in the first session. The features of the bills mentioned above and the issues that most commonly arose in legislative debate are described below.

Legislative History of the Refuge, 2005-2006

As explained below, the ANWR debate took two basic legislative routes in the 109th Congress: (1) budget resolutions and reconciliation bills (S.Con.Res. 18, H.Con.Res. 95, S. 1932, H.R. 4241, S.Con.Res. 83, and H.Con.Res. 376), which cannot be filibustered; and (2) other bills (H.R. 6, an omnibus energy bill; H.R. 2863, Defense appropriations; and H.R. 5429, a bill in the second session to open the Refuge to development), which are subject to filibusters. In none of these measures did Congress reach agreement to allow development.

Budget Resolutions and Reconciliation Bills

The budget resolution and reconciliation were a focus of attention, particularly in the Senate.[9] (See also "Omnibus Energy Legislation," below.) The FY2006 Senate budget resolution (S.Con.Res. 18) passed by the Senate Budget Committee included instructions to the Senate Committee on Energy and Natural Resources to "report changes in laws within its jurisdiction sufficient to reduce outlays by $33,000,000 in FY2006, and $2,658,000,000 for the period of fiscal years 2006 through 2010." The resolution assumed that the committee would report legislation to open ANWR to development, and that leasing would generate $2.5 billion in revenues for the federal government over five years. Senator Cantwell offered a floor amendment (S.Amdt. 168) on March 16, 2005, to remove these instructions. The amendment was defeated (yeas 49, nays 51, Roll Call #52). The FY2006 House budget resolution (H.Con.Res. 95, H.Rept. 109-17), while instructing the House Resources Committee to provide somewhat smaller reductions in outlays, did not include specific assumptions about ANWR revenues.

In the end, the conference agreement (H.Con.Res. 95, H.Rept. 109-62) approved by the House and Senate on April 28, 2005, contained reductions in spending targets of $2.4 billion over FY2006 to FY2010 for the House Resources and Senate Energy Committees that would be difficult to achieve unless ANWR development legislation were passed. The inclusion of the Senate target particularly set the stage for including ANWR development legislation in a reconciliation bill, since reconciliation bills cannot be filibustered (i.e., they require only a simple majority, rather than 60 votes to stop a filibuster).

Under the Congressional Budget Act of 1974 (CBA, Titles I-IX of P.L. 93-344, as amended, 2 U.S.C. §§601-688), while the target reductions of the budget resolutions are binding on the committees, the associated assumptions are not. The Senate Energy and Natural Resources Committee did choose to meet its target by recommending ANWR legislation, and the Budget Committee incorporated the recommendation as Title IV of S. 1932, the Deficit Reduction Act of 2005. There was some question procedurally as to whether Senate rules would permit ANWR legislation to be part of a reconciliation bill.[10] The House Resources Committee included ANWR development legislation, and other spending reductions and offsetting collections, thereby more than meeting the Committee's targets. These measures were incorporated by the House Budget Committee into an omnibus reconciliation bill (H.R. 4241). However, before the House bill came to the floor, considerable opposition to the ANWR provision developed among a number of Republicans, 24 of whom signed a letter to the Speaker opposing its inclusion. The provision was removed before floor consideration; S. 1932 (with the text of H.R. 4241 inserted in lieu — i.e., minus an ANWR provision) passed the House on November 18, 2005 (yeas 217, nays 215; Roll Call #601). ANWR was a major issue in conference. In the end, the conference report (H.Rept. 109-362) omitted ANWR development provisions. The President signed the measure on February 8, 2006 (P.L. 109-171).

The Senate passed the FY2007 budget resolution (S.Con.Res. 83; yeas 51, nays 49, Roll Call #74; no written report) on March 16, 2006. Its sole reconciliation instruction (§201) directed the Committee on Energy and Natural Resources to reduce budget authority by an amount equal to predicted bonus bids, royalties, and rental revenues from ANWR development. According to press reports, some Senators hoped that if the final budget resolution had such instructions — on this topic alone — there would be (1) a FY2007 reconciliation bill on ANWR alone; and (2) sufficient bipartisan support for this single-purpose reconciliation bill in the House to counterbalance opposition of the 24 Republican Members who opposed its inclusion in a much larger FY2006 reconciliation measure in the first session. The FY2007 budget resolution as passed by the House on May 18, 2006, did not include any such instruction (H.Con.Res. 376, H.Rept. 109-402; yeas 218, nays 210, Roll Call #158). The Senate and House, however, did not complete action on the FY2007 budget resolution, and therefore, neither chamber developed or considered any subsequent reconciliation legislation.

ANWR in the Defense Appropriations Bill

As Congress moved toward the December recess, and the chance of an agreement on reconciliation with an ANWR provision seemed to fade, Senator Stevens (Chair of the Defense Appropriations Subcommittee) added an ANWR development title to the "mustpass" FY2006 Defense appropriations bill (H.R. 2863) during conference. Senators opposing ANWR were forced to choose between filibuster of the popular measure or acquiescing to opening the Refuge. Members began a filibuster, and a cloture motion failed (yeas 56, nays 44, Roll Call #364). While the conference report was approved, the relevant two Divisions (C and D) were removed through House and Senate passage of S.Con.Res. 74, correcting the enrollment of the bill (P.L. 109-148).

Omnibus and Other Energy Legislation

The House Resources Committee considered and marked up its portion of the omnibus energy bill on April 13, 2005, before the bill was introduced. The provisions, including an ANWR development title, were approved by the committee and incorporated into the House version of H.R. 6 and introduced by Representative Barton (Chair of the Energy and Commerce Committee) on April 18. During House consideration on April 20, Representatives Markey and Johnson offered an amendment (H.Amdt. 73) to strike the title; it was rejected (yeas 200, nays 231, Roll Call #122). The House passed H.R. 6 on April 21 (yeas 249, nays 183, Roll Call #132). The Senate passed its version of H.R. 6 on June 28, 2005 (yeas 85, nays 12, Roll Call #158). The Senate bill contained no ANWR development provisions. The ANWR title was omitted in the final measure (P.L. 109-58).

On May 25, 2006, the House passed H.R. 5429, to open ANWR to development (yeas 225, nays 201, Roll Call #209). In nearly all respects, the bill was similar to the ANWR title in the House version of H.R. 6. (See "Major Legislative Issues," below, for details.) The bill was not taken up by the Senate.

Major Legislative Issues in the 107th, 108th, and 109th Congresses

Some of the issues that have been raised most frequently in the ANWR debate are described briefly below. In addition to the issue of whether development should be permitted at all, key aspects of the debate include restrictions that might be specified in legislation, including the physical size, or footprint, of development; the regulation of activities on Native lands; the disposition of revenues; labor issues; oil export restrictions; compliance with the National Environmental Policy Act; and other matters. (References below to the "Secretary" refer to the Secretary of the Interior, unless stated otherwise.)

107th Congress

H.R. 4, as passed by the House, was the model for two Senate amendments (S.Amdt. 3132 and S.Amdt. 3133), with some important variations. With brief background information for each topic, H.R. 4 is analyzed below, along with a few of the major features of the rejected Senate amendments to S. 517 (where these differ significantly from H.R. 4), and the two wilderness bills.[11]

108th Congress

The analysis below describe features of H.R. 6 as passed by the House and H.R. 4514 (identical, except as noted in "Revenue Disposition," below). S. 2095 and the Senate version of H.R. 6 had no provision to develop the 1002 area, but any provisions corresponding to issues below are also described.

109th Congress

The analysis below describes H.R. 5429 as passed by the House; the provisions of Division C of the conference report on H.R. 2863 (the "Defense bill"), and §4001 of S. 1932, the Senate reconciliation bill (the "Senate bill"). Because of the lack of detail in §4001, many aspects of ANWR leasing would have been left to administrative decisions, with levels of public participation in some instances curtailed along with judicial review, as noted below.

Environmental Direction

Should Congress open the Refuge to energy leasing, it could choose to leave environmental matters to administrative agencies under existing laws.

Alternatively, Congress could impose a higher standard of environmental protection because the area is in a national wildlife refuge or because of the fragility of the arctic environment, or it could legislate a lower standard to facilitate development. The degree of discretion given to the administering agency could also affect the stringency of environmental protection. For example, Congress could include provisions requiring use of "the best available technology" or "the best commercially available technology" or similar general standards; alternatively, it could limit judicial review of environmental standards. Another issue would be the use of gravel and water resources essential for oil exploration and development. Congress could also leave environmental protection largely up to the administering agency — to be accomplished through regulations, or through lease stipulations. The former require public notice and comment, while the latter do not involve public participation, and may provide fewer public enforcement options. Other legislative issues include limitations on miles of roads or other surface occupancy; the adequacy of existing pollution standards; prevention and treatment of spills; the adequacy of current environmental requirements; and aircraft overflights, among other things.

107th Congress

H.R. 4 (§6507(a)) required the Secretary to administer a leasing program so as to "result in no significant adverse effect on fish and wildlife, their habitat, subsistence resources, and the environment, ... including ... requiring the application of the best commercially available technology...." H.R. 4 (§6503(a)(2)) would have also required that this program be done "in a manner that ensures the receipt of fair market value by the public for the mineral resources to be leased." It is unclear how the two goals of environmental protection and of fair market value related to each other (e.g., if environmental restrictions might make some fields uneconomic). H.R. 4 (§6506(a)(3) and (5)) would have required lessees to be responsible and liable for reclamation of lands within the Coastal Plain to support pre-leasing uses or to a higher use approved by the Secretary. There were requirements for mitigation, development of regulations by DOI, and other measures to protect the environment. These included prohibitions on public access to service roads and other transportation restrictions. Other provisions could also have affected environmental protection. H.R. 770 and S. 411 would have designated the area as wilderness, as discussed below.

108th Congress

The House bill did not name a lead agency, but since §30403(a) stated that the program would be administered under the Mineral Leasing Act, BLM seemed likely to lead. The House bill (§30407(a)) required the Secretary to administer the leasing program so as to "result in no significant adverse effect on fish and wildlife, their habitat, and the environment, [and to require] the application of the best commercially available technology...." The House bill (§30403(a)(2)) also required that this program be done "in a manner that ensures the receipt of fair market value by the public for the mineral resources to be leased." It is unclear how the two goals of environmental protection and of fair market value were to relate to each other (e.g., if environmental restrictions might make some fields uneconomic). As in the 107th Congress, the House bill (§§30406(a)(3) and (5)) was identical to §§6506(a)(3) and (5) in the 107th Congress. H.R. 770 and S. 543 would have designated the area as wilderness, as discussed below.

109th Congress

H.R. 5429 named BLM as the lead agency. Section 7(a) required the Secretary to administer the leasing program so as to "result in no significant adverse effect on fish and wildlife, their habitat, and the environment, [and to require] the application of the best commercially available technology...." Section 3(a)(2) would also have required that this program be done "in a manner that ensures the receipt of fair market value by the public for the mineral resources to be leased." It is unclear how the two goals of environmental protection and fair market value would have related to each other (e.g., if environmental restrictions would have made some fields uneconomic). Subsections 6(a)(3) and (5) required lessees to be responsible and liable for reclamation of lands within the Coastal Plain (unless the Secretary approved other arrangements), and required that the lands support preleasing uses or a higher use approved by the Secretary. There were requirements for mitigation, development of regulations, and other measures to protect the environment. These included prohibitions on public access to service roads and other transportation restrictions. Other provisions might also have affected environmental protection. (See "Judicial Review," below.) The Defense bill (§7) was similar to the House bill. The Senate bill (§4001(b)(1)(B)) directed the Secretary to establish and implement an "environmentally sound" leasing system, but did not provide further direction.

The Size of Footprints — Federal Lands

Newer technologies permit greater consolidation of leasing operations, which tends to reduce the size and the environmental impacts of development. One aspect of the debate in Congress has focused on the size of footprints in the development and production phases of energy leasing. The term *footprint* does not have a universally accepted definition, and therefore the types of structures falling under a "footprint restriction" are arguable (e.g., the inclusion of exploratory structures, roads, gravel mines, port facilities, etc.)[12] In addition, it is unclear whether exploratory structures or structures on Native lands would be included under any provision limiting footprints.[13] The new map accompanying S. 1932 in the 109th Congress included the Native lands in its definition of the Coastal Plain leasing area, but how the federal leasing program would have applied to those lands was not clear. (See "New Maps," below.)

Development advocates have emphasized the total acreage of surface disturbance, while opponents have emphasized the dispersal of not only the structures themselves but also their impacts over much of the 1.5 million acres of the 1002 area. One single consolidated facility of 2,000 acres (3.1 square miles, a limit currently supported by some development advocates) would not permit full development of the 1002 area. Instead, full development of the 1002 area would require that facilities, even if limited to 2,000 acres in total surface area, be widely dispersed. Dispersal is necessary due to the limits of lateral (or extended reach) drilling: the current North Slope record for this technology is 4 miles. If that record were matched on all sides of a single pad, at most about 4% of the Coastal Plain could be developed from that pad. If the current world record (7 miles) were matched, about 11% of the 1002 area could be accessed from a single compact 2,000-acre facility. In addition, drilling opponents argue that energy facilities have impacts on recreation, subsistence, vegetation, and wildlife well beyond areas actually covered by development.

107th Congress

H.R. 4 (§6507(d)(9)) provided for consolidation of leasing operations; among other things, consolidation would tend to reduce environmental impacts of development. H.R. 4 (§6507(a)(3)) would have gone further to require, "consistent with the provisions of section 6503" (which included ensuring receipt of fair market value), that the Secretary administer the leasing program to "ensure that the maximum amount of surface acreage covered by production and support facilities, including airstrips and any areas covered by gravel berms or piers for the support of pipelines, does not exceed 2,000 acres on the Coastal Plain." A floor amendment to H.R. 4 with this acreage restriction was passed on August 1, 2001 (yeas 228, nays 201; Roll Call #316). The terms used were not defined in the bill (nor discussed in the committee report), and therefore the full set of structures that might have fallen under the restriction was arguable (e.g., whether roads, gravel mines, and structures on Native lands would be included under this provision). Floor debate focused on the extent to which the facilities covered in the amendment would be widely distributed around the Refuge. The acreage limitation appeared not to apply to Native lands.

108ᵗʰ Congress

The House bill (§30407(d)(9)) provided for consolidation of leasing operations in language identical to that in the 107ᵗʰ Congress. A floor amendment by Representative Wilson (NM) to the House bill with an identical 2000-acre limit was passed on April 10, 2003 (yeas 226, nays 202; Roll Call #134). Floor debate focused on the extent to which the facilities would be widely distributed around the Refuge. In addition, Native lands might not have been limited by this provision. (See "Native Lands," below.)

109ᵗʰ Congress

H.R. 5429 (§7(d)(9)) provided for consolidation of leasing operations to reduce environmental impacts of development. Section §7(a)(3) would have further required, "consistent with the provisions of section 3" (which included ensuring receipt of fair market value for mineral resources), that the Secretary administer the leasing program to "ensure that the maximum amount of surface acreage covered by production and support facilities, including airstrips and any areas covered by gravel berms or piers for the support of pipelines, does not exceed 2,000 acres on the Coastal Plain." The terms used were not defined in the bill and therefore the range of structures which would have been covered by the restriction is arguable (e.g., whether roads, gravel mines, causeways, and water treatment plants would be included under this provision). In addition, the wording may not have applied to structures built during the exploratory phase. An essentially identical provision was in S. 1932

($4001(f)) and H.R. 2863 ($7(a)(3)). H.R. 2863 also called for facility consolidation ($7(d)(4)) and for the Secretary to develop a consolidation plan ($7(f)).

Native Lands

Generally, the Alaska Natives (Inuit) along the North Slope have supported ANWR development, while the Natives of interior Alaska (Gwich'in) have opposed it, though neither group is unanimous. ANCSA resolved aboriginal claims against the United States by (among other things) creating Village Corporations that could select surface lands, and Regional Corporations that could select surface and subsurface rights as well. Kaktovik Inupiat Village (KIC) selected surface lands (originally approximately three townships) on the coastal plain of ANWR but these KIC lands were administratively excluded from being considered as within the administratively defined "1002 Coastal Plain." A fourth township was added by ANCILA, and is within the defined Coastal Plain. The four townships, totaling approximately 92,000 acres, are all within the Refuge and subject to its regulations. The Arctic Slope Regional Corporation (ASRC) obtained subsurface rights beneath the KIC lands pursuant to a 1983 land exchange agreement. In addition, there are currently thousands of acres of conveyed or claimed individual Native allotments in the 1002 area of the Refuge that are not expressly subject to its regulations. Were oil and gas development authorized for the federal lands in the Refuge, development would then be allowed or become feasible on the nearly 100,000 acres of Native lands, possibly free of any acreage limitation applying to development on the federal lands, depending on how legislation is framed. The extent to which the Native lands could be regulated to protect the environment is uncertain, given the status of allotments and some of the language in the 1983 agreement with ASRC.[14] (See "New Maps," below.)

107th Congress

H.R. 4 would have repealed the ANILCA prohibition on oil and gas development. If oil and gas development were authorized for the federal lands in the Refuge, it appears that development could occur on the more than 100,000 acres of Native lands, arguably free of any acreage limitation applying to development on the federal lands. The extent to which the Native lands could be regulated to protect the environment is uncertain, given the status of allotments and some of the language in the 1983 agreement with ASRC.[15] After the cloture vote on S.Amdt. 3132 on April 18, 2002, Senator Stevens publicly stated his intent to offer an amendment to open Native lands in this part of the Refuge to energy development, but he did not do so.

108th Congress

The House bill would have repealed the ANILCA prohibition on oil and gas development. (See preceding paragraph.)

109th Congress

See "New Maps," below.

New Maps

Both the House and Senate have created new maps of the "Coastal Plain" that would be the subject of leasing.[16] The Coastal Plain was defined in §1002 of ANILCA as the area indicated on an August 1980 map. The 1980 map is now missing. An administrative articulation of the boundary was authorized by §103(b) of ANILCA and has the force of law. Since the 1980 map is missing, evaluating whether the administrative description properly excluded the Native Lands is impossible, and, as noted, the fourth Native Township (selected later) is not excluded from the Coastal Plain by that description. The legal description required under ANILCA was completed in 1983 (48 *Fed, Reg.*16838, Apr. 19, 1983; 50 C.F.R. Part 37, App. I), but questions also surround this description.[17] The description excluded three Native townships from the articulated Coastal Plain. Some bills in various Congresses also have excluded these same Native lands by referring to the 1980 map and the administrative description.

109th Congress.[18]

S. 1932 (§4001(a)) provided a new map, dated September 2005, to accompany its submission to the Budget Committee for reconciliation. This map included *all* Native lands in the "Coastal Plain."[19] However, the bill text did not refer to the Native lands, and the extent of federal control of Native lands that was intended or accomplished by the map change is not clear. For example, the bill directed a 50/50 revenue split between the State of Alaska and the federal government, thereby possibly giving rise to Native claims for compensation for revenues from their lands. If this revenue provision was not intended to apply to Native lands, it was not clear whether other provisions also might not apply. Also, some of the terms in the 1983 Agreement with ASRC call for an express congressional override to negate some of its terms, and the text of the bill did not discuss the Native lands or the Agreement. The Defense bill also used a USGS map dated September 2005 (§2(4)); it is not clear whether the map is the same as the one referred to in the Senate bill.

H.R. 5429 did not refer to a map, but instead defined the Coastal Plain as the area described in 50 C.F.R. Part 37, App. I (the administrative articulation of the Coastal Plain). As discussed, this regulation currently excludes three Native townships, but leaves the fourth within the Coastal Plain, and arguably the leasing provisions would have applied to it. The House bill raised the possibility that the defined Coastal Plain could be expanded or reduced at some later time through rulemaking procedures.

Revenue Disposition

Another issue is whether Congress may validly provide for a disposition of revenues according to a formula other than the (essentially) 90% state - 10% federal split specified in the Alaska Statehood Act. A court in *Alaska v. United States* (35 Fed. Cl. 685, 701 (1996)) indicated that the language in the Statehood Act means that Alaska is to be treated like other states for federal leasing *conducted under the Mineral Leasing Act* (MLA), which contains (basically) a 90% -10% split. Arguably, Congress can establish a different, *non-MLA* leasing regimen with a different ratio — for example, the separate leasing arrangements that govern the National Petroleum Reserve-Alaska, where the revenue-sharing formula is 50/50 — but this issue was not before the court and hence remains an open issue.[20]

In the past, a number of ANWR bills have specified the disposition of the federal portion of the revenues. Among the spending purposes have been federal land acquisition, energy research, and federal assistance to local governments in Alaska to mitigate the impact of energy development. Amounts would have been either permanently or annually appropriated. In the latter case, there would be little practical distinction between annually appropriating funds based on ANWR revenues and annually appropriating funds from the General Treasury. If there is no particular purpose specified for leasing revenues, the resulting revenues would be deposited in the Treasury where they would be available for any general government use.

107ᵗʰ Congress

Several sections of H.R. 4 related to revenues. Section 6512 would have provided that 50% of adjusted revenues be paid to Alaska. Then 50% of revenues from bonus payments were to go into a Renewable Energy Technology Investment Fund; and 50% from rents and royalties were to go into a Royalties Conservation Fund. It is not clear whether the basis for the shared revenues was to be gross or net receipts. More fundamentally, under §6503(a), the Secretary was to establish and implement a leasing program *under the Mineral Leasing Act*, yet §6512 directed a revenue sharing program different from that in the MLA. Establishing a leasing program under the MLA, yet providing for a different revenue disposition could have raised additional questions of legal validity. If the alternative disposition were struck down and the revenue provisions were determined to be severable, it is possible that Alaska could have received 90% of the revenues from ANWR.

108ᵗʰ Congress

Several sections of the House bill related to revenues. Section 30409 would have provided that 50% of adjusted revenues be paid to Alaska, and the balance deposited in the U.S. Treasury as miscellaneous receipts, except for the portion allocated to a fund to assist Alaska communities in addressing local impacts of energy development under §30412. The assistance fund was not to exceed $11 million in an unspent balance, with $5 million available for annual appropriation. Section 30403(a) was identical to §6503(a) (establishing a leasing program under the MLA) in the 107ᵗʰ Congress. In addition, in the House version of H.R. 6, §30409(c) would have allowed certain revenues from bids for leasing to be appropriated for energy assistance for low-income households. This provision was lacking in H.R. 4514 — the only difference between the two bills.

109ᵗʰ Congress

Under §3(a) of H.R. 5429, the Secretary was to establish and implement a leasing program for ANWR in accordance with the bill, and §9 stated that "notwithstanding any other provision of law," revenues were to be shared 50/50 between the federal government and Alaska (with some special provisions on the federal share). It can be argued that the leasing program is not "under the MLA" and hence the different revenue-sharing provisions were not contrary to the Alaska Statehood Act. However, if a court struck down the revenue-sharing provision, it would then have to determine if that provision was *severable* — whether Congress would have enacted the rest of the statute without the flawed provision. H.R. 5429 did not have a "severability" provision that stated the intent of Congress in this regard. If a court both struck down the revenue-sharing provision and found it to be severable, then Alaska could receive 90% of ANWR revenues.

Similarly, S. 1932 also did not state that leasing would be under the MLA, and also set out many requirements that differed from those of the MLA. "Notwithstanding any other provision of law," it too directed that receipts from leasing and operations "authorized under this section" be divided equally between the state of Alaska and the federal government. Because of the change in the Senate definition of *Coastal Plain* and the accompanying map, the bill might have included revenues from Native lands in the 50/50 split. The Defense bill (Division D, §1) also provided for a 50/50 split, and contained various provisions for distribution of certain percentages of the federal share to various purposes, including hurricane relief. In addition, §14 of Division C of the Defense bill contained a severability provision that provided explicitly that if any portion of either Division C or D were held to be *unconstitutional*, the remainder of the two divisions would not be affected. It is not clear to what provisions the severability language might have applied. As discussed, some issues regarding the revenue split might remain, but those issues might rest on contractual interpretations, rather than constitutional concerns. However, if the 50/50 revenue split were struck down, Alaska could receive 90% of the ANWR revenues and, if so, fewer federal funds would be available for programs premised on the 50% federal share.

Natural Gas Pipeline

Significant quantities of natural gas are known to exist in the developed oil fields on the North Slope, but cannot be sold elsewhere for lack of transportation. If a natural gas pipeline were constructed from these fields, any natural gas in ANWR might become economic as well. A decision to construct a pipeline to transport natural gas from Alaska to North American markets entails risk as well as a decision on the route.

107th Congress

The Senate version of H.R. 4 attempted to address the pipeline by providing federal guarantees for loans to construct a natural gas transport system. Guarantees were not to exceed 80% of a loan; and the total loan principal to which guarantees apply was not to exceed $10 billion. The Senate bill also provided for a tax credit for the production of Alaska North Slope gas that effectively established a price floor of $3.25 per thousand cubic feet. Both the House and the Senate versions addressed the route issue by prohibiting the licensing of a route that enters Canada north of 68° latitude. Canadian energy industry interests objected to the prohibition of the northern route through Canada (a southern route would bypass gas reserves in far northwest Canada), and they said that the tax credit would have given Alaskan gas producers a price advantage over Canadian producers.

108th Congress

The Senate's revised bill, S. 2095, provided a loan guarantee not to exceed 80% of the total capital cost of the project, nor to exceed $18 billion (indexed for inflation), and had a tax credit mechanism that effectively would guarantee a minimum price for natural gas transported through the pipeline. The House's H.R. 6 would have provided no means of reducing risk nor other economic incentive to build. Regarding the route, the House bill, both Senate bills, and the conference on H.R. 6 report prohibited the licensing of a route that enters Canada north of 68° latitude. Canadian energy interests opposed a production tax credit for Alaskan gas producers, which would tend to give a price advantage over Canadian producers. They also objected to the prohibition of a northern route through Canada because a southern route would bypass gas reserves in far northwest Canada. In fact, Canadian interests are moving to build a pipeline from that area.[21]

109th Congress

Because of actions in the 108th Congress, this issue was not raised in the 109th Congress.

Project Labor Agreements (PLAs)

A recurring issue in federal and federally funded projects is whether project owners or contractors should be required, by agreement, to use union workers. PLAs are agreements between a project owner or main contractor and the union(s) representing craft workers that establish the terms and conditions of work that will apply for the particular project. The agreement may also specify a source (such as a union hiring hall) to supply the craft workers. Typically, the agreement is binding on all contractors and subcontractors working on the project, and specifies wage rates and benefits, discusses procedures for resolving labor and jurisdictional disputes, and includes a no-strike clause. Proponents of PLAs, including construction and other unions, argue that PLAs ensure a reliable, efficient labor source, help keep costs down, and ensure access for union members to federal and federally funded projects. Opponents, including nonunion firms and their supporters, believe that PLAs inflate costs, reduce competition, and unfairly restrict access to those projects. There is little independent information to weigh the validity of the conflicting assertions.

107th Congress

H.R. 4 (§6506) directed the Secretary to require lessees "to negotiate to obtain a project labor agreement." The Secretary was to do so "recognizing the Government's proprietary interest in labor stability and the ability of construction labor and management to meet the particular needs and conditions of projects to be developed ...." In §714 of the Senate-passed version of H.R. 4, the Senate "urges" the sponsors of any pipeline project to carry natural gas south to U.S. or Canadian markets from North Slope development (on or off the Refuge) "to negotiate a project labor agreement to expedite construction of the pipeline."

108th Congress

The House's H.R. 6 contained the same requirement for a PLA. The gas pipeline provisions in the House and Senate bills both urged the sponsors of the pipeline project "to negotiate a project labor agreement to expedite construction of the pipeline."

109th Congress

H.R. 5429 (§6(b)) directed the Secretary to require lessees in the 1002 area to "negotiate to obtain a project labor agreement" — "recognizing the Government's proprietary interest in labor stability and the ability of construction labor and management to meet the particular needs and conditions of projects to be developed...." H.R. 2863 (§6(b)) contained similar provisions, but S. 1932 had no similar provision.

Oil Export Restrictions

Export of North Slope oil in general, and any ANWR oil in particular, has been an issue, beginning at least with the authorization of the TransAlaska Pipeline (TAPS) in 1973, and continuing into the current ANWR debate. Much of the TAPS route is on federal lands and the MLA prohibits export of oil transported through pipelines granted rights-of-way over federal lands (16 U.S.C. §185(u)). The Trans-Alaska Pipeline Authorization Act (P.L. 93-153, 43 U.S.C. §1651 et seq.), specified that oil shipped through it could be exported only under restrictive conditions. Subsequent legislation strengthened the export restrictions further.[22] Oil began to be shipped through the pipeline in increasing amounts as North Slope oilfield development grew in the 1970s and 1980s. With exports effectively banned, most of the North Slope oil went to West Coast destinations; the rest was shipped to the Gulf Coast via the Panama Canal or overland across the isthmus. In the early and mid-1990s, the combination of California, North Slope, and federal offshore production, plus imports, produced large crude oil supplies relative to demand. California prices fell, causing complaints from California and North Slope producers.

By 1995, several years of low world oil prices and relative calm in the Mideast had reduced concern about petroleum supplies. Market forces eventually created pressure to change the law. In 1995, P.L. 104-58 (30 U.S.C. §185(s)) was enacted, Title II of which amended the MLA to provide that oil transported through TAPS may be exported unless the President finds, after considering stated criteria, that it is *not* in the national interest. North Slope exports rose to a peak of 74,000 barrels/day in 1999, representing 7% of North Slope production. North Slope oil exports ceased voluntarily in May 2000 and have since been minimal, as Alaska producers found adequate U.S. markets at world prices.

If Congress wished to limit export of any oil from the 1002 area, by applying the restriction to oil transported through TAPS, the restriction might not be effective: oil shipment via tanker could become practical if current warming trends in the Arctic continue and if crude oil prices provide sufficient incentive. Recent proposed bans on export of ANWR oil have not been tied to shipment through TAPS.

107th Congress

H.R. 4 (§6506 (a)(8)) would have required the Secretary to prohibit export of oil produced under a lease in the 1002 area as a condition of a lease.

108th Congress

The House bill (§30406(a)(8)) would have required the prohibition on the export of oil produced in the 1002 area as a condition of a lease.

109th Congress

H.R. 5429 (§6(a)(8)) would have prohibited the export of oil produced in the 1002 area as a condition of a lease. S. 1932 (§4001(g)) contained a similar provision, as did H.R. 2863 (§12). However, inasmuch as other North Slope oil is allowed to be exported, it would appear that prohibiting the export of ANWR oil could be moot: producers aiming to tap the export market would substitute other North Slope oil to meet the demand.

NEPA Compliance

The National Environmental Policy Act of 1969 (NEPA, P.L. 91-190; 42 U.S.C. §4321) requires the preparation of an environmental impact statement (EIS) to examine the effects of major federal actions with significant effects on the environment, and to provide public involvement in agency decisions. The last full EIS examining the effects of energy development in ANWR was the Final Legislative Environmental Impact Statement (FLEIS) completed in 1987, and some observers assert that a new EIS is needed to support development now. NEPA requires an EIS to analyze an array of alternatives, including a "no action" alternative. Some development supporters would like to see the process truncated, in light of past analyses and to hasten production. Development opponents, and NEPA supporters, argue that the 19-year gap and changed circumstances since the last analysis necessitates a thorough update, and stress the flaws they found in the 1987 FLEIS.

107th Congress

Both bills addressed the issue. H.R. 4 (§6503(c)) deemed the 1987 FLEIS adequate with respect to actions by the Secretary to develop leasing regulations, yet required the Secretary to prepare an EIS with respect to other actions, some of which might require only a (usually shorter) "environmental assessment." Consideration of alternatives was to be limited to two choices: a preferred option and a "single leasing alternative." (Generally, an EIS analyzes a range of alternatives, including a "no action" alternative.)

108th Congress

Section 30403(c) of the House bill had the same provisions on NEPA compliance.

109th Congress

Section 3(c) of the H.R. 5429 deemed the 1987 FLEIS tosatisfy NEPA requirements with respect to prelease activities and the development and promulgation of leasing regulations, and required the Secretary to prepare an EIS of all other actions authorized by the subtitle before the first lease sale. Consideration of alternatives was to be limited to two choices, a preferred leasing action and a "single leasing alternative." Compliance with the subsection was deemed to satisfy all requirements to analyze the environmental effects of proposed leasing. H.R. 2863 (Division C , §3(c)) was essentially identical. S. 1932 (§4001(c)) had similar provisions, but did not expressly require an EIS for leasing.

Compatibility with Refuge Purposes

Under current law for the management of national wildlife refuges (16 U.S.C.§668dd), and under 43 C.F.R. §3101.5-3 for Alaskan refuges specifically, an activity may be allowed in a refuge only if it is compatible with the purposes of the particular Refuge and with those of the Refuge System as a whole.

107th Congress

H.R. 4 (§6503(c)) stated that the oil and gas leasing program and activities in the Coastal Plain were deemed to be compatible with the purposes for which ANWR was established and that no further findings or decisions were required to implement this determination. This language appeared intended to answer the compatibility question and to eliminate the usual compatibility determination processes. The general statement that leasing "activities" are compatible arguably encompassed necessary support activities such as construction and operation of port facilities, staging areas, personnel centers, etc.

108th Congress

Section 30403(c) of the House bill had the same provisions as in the 107th Congress.

109th Congress

Section 3(c) of the H.R. 5429, §3(c) of H.R. 2863, and §4001(c) of S. 1932 stated that the energy leasing program and activities in the coastal plain were deemed to be compatible with the purposes for which ANWR was established and that no further findings or decisions were required to implement this determination. This language appeared to eliminate the usual compatibility determination processes. The extent of leasing "activities" that might have been included as compatible is debatable and arguably might encompass necessary support activities, such as construction and operation of port facilities, staging areas, and personnel centers.

Judicial Review

Leasing proponents urge that any ANWR leasing program be put in place promptly and argue that expediting, curtailing, or prohibiting judicial review is desirable to achieve that goal. Judicial review can be expedited through procedural changes, such as reducing the time limits within which suits must be filed, avoiding some level of review, curtailing the scope of the review, or increasing the burden imposed on challengers. In the past, bills before Congress have combined various elements.

107th Congress

H.R. 4 contemplated prompt action to put a leasing program in place and had sections on expedited judicial review. H.R. 4 would have required that complaints be filed within 90 days. H.R. 4 (§§6508(a)(1) and (2)) appeared to contradict each other as to where suits were to be filed and it is possible part of a sentence was omitted. H.R. 4 (§6508(a)(3)) would also have limited the scope of review by stating that review of a Secretarial decision, including environmental analyses, was to be limited to whether the Secretary complied with the terms of Division F of H.R. 4, be based on the administrative record, and that the Secretary's analysis of environmental effects was "presumed to be correct unless shown otherwise by clear and convincing evidence to the contrary." This standard in this context arguably would make overturning a decision more difficult.

108th Congress

The House bill (§30408) had the same provisions as in the 107th Congress.

109th Congress

H.R. 5429 (§8) required that any complaints seeking judicial review be filed within 90 days. Section 8(a)(2) provided that suits were to be filed in the Court of Appeals in Washington, DC, as did H.R. 2863 (§8(a)). H.R. 5429 (§8(a)(3)) would also have limited the scope of review by stating that review of a secretarial decision, including environmental analyses, would be limited to whether the Secretary complied with the terms of the ANWR subtitle, that it would be based on the administrative record, and that the Secretary's analysis of environmental effects is "presumed to be correct unless shown otherwise by clear and convincing evidence to the contrary." This standard is unclear, but in this context arguably would make overturning a decision more difficult. S. 1932 and H.R. 2863 (§4001(c) and §8(a), respectively) were similar. S. 1932 omitted the presumption concerning the Secretary's analysis of environmental effects.

Special Areas

Some have supported setting aside certain areas in the coastal plain for protection of their ecological or cultural values. This could be done by designating the areas specifically in legislation, or by authorizing the Secretary to set aside areas to be selected after enactment. The FLEIS identified four special areas that together total more than 52,000 acres. The Secretary could be required to restrict or prevent development in these areas or any others that may seem significant, or to select among areas if an acreage limitation on such set-asides is imposed.

107th Congress

H.R. 4 (§6503(e)) allowed the Secretary to set aside up to 45,000 acres of special areas, and named one specific area in which leases, if permitted, would forbid surface occupancy. As mentioned above, the FLEIS identified four special areas which together total more than 52,000 acres, so the Secretary would have been required to select among these areas or any others that may seem significant. H.R. 770 and S. 411 would have designated the entire 1002 area as wilderness.

108th Congress

The House bill (§30403(e)) had the same provisions as in the 107th Congress. Section 30403(f) also stated that the closure authority in the ANWR title was to be the Secretary's sole authority, which might limit possible secretarial actions under the Endangered Species Act (P.L.93-205; 16 U.S.C. §1531ff). H.R. 770 and S. 543 would have designated the entire 1002 area as wilderness.

109th Congress

H.R. 5429 (§3(e)) allowed the Secretary to set aside up to 45,000 acres (and names one specific special area) in which leases, if permitted, would forbid surface occupancy. Because the four special areas are larger than this total, the Secretary would be required to select among these areas or any others that may seem significant. Section 3(f) also stated that the closure authority in the ANWR title was to be the Secretary's sole authority, which might limit possible secretarial actions under the Endangered Species Act. H.R. 2863 (§3(e)) was essentially identical. S. 2863 had no provision for special areas.

Non-Development Options

Several options have been available to Congress to either postpone or forbid development, unless Congress were later to change the law. These options are allowing exploration only, designating the 1002 area as wilderness, and taking no action. The legislative history of these options is described below.

Exploration Only

Some have argued that the 1002 area should be opened to exploration first, before a decision is made on whether to proceed to leasing. Those with this view hold that with greater certainty about the presence or absence of energy resources, a better decision could be made about whether to open the coastal plain for full leasing. This idea has had relatively little support over the years. For those opposed to energy development, the reasons are fairly clear: if exploration results in no or insufficient economic discoveries, any damage from exploration would remain. If there were economic discoveries, support for further development might be unstoppable. Those who support development see unacceptable risks in such a proposal. First, who would be charged with carrying out exploration, who would pay for it, and to whom would the results be available? Second, if no economic discoveries were made, would that be because the "best" places (in the eyes of whatever observer) were not examined? Third, might any small discoveries become economic in the future? Fourth, if discoveries did occur, could industry still be foreclosed from development, or might sparse but promising data elevate bidding to unreasonable levels? Fifth, if exploration is authorized, what provisions, if any, should pertain to Native lands? In short, various advocates see insufficient gain from such a proposal, and it has not been introduced in recent years.

Wilderness Designation

Energy development is not permitted in wilderness areas, unless there are valid pre-existing rights or unless Congress specifically allows it or later reverses the designation. Development of the surface and subsurface holdings of Native corporations would be precluded inside wilderness boundaries (though compensation might be owed). It would also preserve existing recreational opportunities and jobs, as well as the existing level of protection of subsistence resources, including the Porcupine Caribou Herd.

107th Congress. H.R. 770 and S. 411 would have designated the 1002 area as wilderness.

108th Congress. H.R. 770 and S. 543 would have designated the 1002 area as wilderness.

109th Congress. H.R. 567 and S. 261 would have designated the 1002 area as part of the National Wilderness System.

Presidential Certification

Under the two Senate amendments to S. 517 in the 107th Congress (which were ultimately rejected by the Senate), the leasing provisions would have taken effect upon a determination and certification by the President that development of the Coastal Plain is in the national economic and security interests of the United States. This determination and certification were to be in the sole discretion of the President and would not be reviewable. This option has not been raised in other bills.

No Action

Because current law prohibits development unless Congress acts, this option also prevents energy development on both federal and Native lands. Those supporting delay often argue that not enough is known about either the probability of discoveries or about the environmental impact if development is permitted. Others argue that oil deposits should be saved for an unspecified "right time."

SELECTED LEGISLATION IN THE 107TH CONGRESS

H.R. 4 (Tauzin)

Division F, Title V, contained the provisions of H.R. 2436, with the inclusion of a new provision for a 50/50 federal/state revenue split. Introduced July 27, 2001; referred to Committees on Energy and Commerce, Science, Ways and Means, Resources, Education and the Workforce, Transportation and Infrastructure, the Budget, and Financial Services. August 1, 2001, House passed Sununu amendment to limit specified surface development to 2,000 acres (yeas 228, nays 201; Roll Call #316) and defeated Markey-Johnson (CT) amendment to strike Title V defeated (yeas 206, nays 223; Roll Call #317). Passed House August 2, 2001 (yeas 240, nays 189; Roll Call #320). House conferees appointed June 12, 2002. Senate struck all after enacting clause and substituted text of S. 517 (amended); passed Senate April 25, 2002 (yeas 88, nays 11; Roll Call #94). Senate appointed conferees May 1, 2002.

H.R. 39 (D. Young)

To repeal current prohibition against ANWR leasing; direct the Secretary to establish competitive oil and gas leasing program; specify that the 1987 FLEIS would be sufficient for compliance with NEPA; authorize set-asides up to 45,000 acres of Special Areas that restrict surface occupancy; set minimum for royalty payments and for tract sizes; and for other purposes. Introduced January 3, 2001; referred to Committee on Resources.

H.R. 770 (Markey)

To designate Arctic coastal plain of ANWR as wilderness. Introduced February 28, 2001; referred to Committee on Resources.

H.R. 2436 (Hansen)

Title V to repeal current prohibition against ANWR leasing; direct Secretary to establish competitive oil and gas leasing program; specify that the

1987 FLEIS would be sufficient for compliance with NEPA; authorize set-asides up to 45,000 acres of Special Areas that restrict surface occupancy; set minimum acreage for the first lease sale and minimum royalty payments; prohibit ANWR oil export; specify project labor agreements; and for other purposes. Introduced July 10, 2001; referred to Committee on Resources and on Energy and Commerce. Reported (amended) by Resources on July 25 (H.Rept. 107-160, Part I) and discharged by Energy and Commerce on July 25, 2001. Provisions incorporated into H.R. 4.

S. 388 (Murkowski)

Title V to open the 1002 area to energy leasing; provide for the timing and size of lease sales; specify that the 1987 FLEIS would be sufficient for compliance with NEPA; require posting of bonds for reclamation; require expedited judicial review; authorize set-asides up to 45,000 acres of Special Areas that restrict surface occupancy; provide for a 50/50 revenue split with the state; require on-site inspections; provide for use of any federal revenues; and other purposes. Introduced February 26, 2001; referred to Committee on Energy and Natural Resources.

S. 411 (Lieberman)

To designate Arctic coastal plain of ANWR as wilderness. Introduced February 28, 2001; referred to Committee on Environment and Public Works.

S. 517 (Bingaman)

To authorize a program for technology transfer in the Department of Energy. Introduced March 12, 2001; referred to Committee on Energy and Natural Resources. Reported June 6, 2001 (S.Rept. 107-30). February 15, 2002, laid before Senate by unanimous consent. February 15, 2002, S.Amdt. 2917 (Daschle) proposed authorizing an omnibus energy program. S.Amdt. 3132 (Murkowski) and S.Amdt. 3133 (Stevens) to open the Refuge to energy development; filed April 16, 2002; S.Amdt. 3133 failed cloture motion (36 yeas to 64 nays; Roll Call #70) and was withdrawn, April 18, 2002. S.Amdt. 3132 failed cloture motion (46 yeas to 54 nays; Roll Call #71) on April 18,

2002. A cloture motion was filed on S. 517 on Apil 18, 2002; cloture invoked April 23 (yeas 86, nays 13; Roll Call #77). Senate incorporated this measure in H.R. 4 as an amendment, April 25, 2002.

S. 1766 (Daschle)

To alter national energy programs in a variety of ways; lacked provisions to open ANWR. Introduced December 5, 2001; not referred to Committee.

SELECTED LEGISLATION IN THE 108TH CONGRESS

H.R. 6 (Tauzin)

Title IV, Division C to repeal current prohibition against ANWR development, create energy leasing program, and provide for distribution of revenues. Introduced April 7, 2003; referred to eight committees, including Committee on Resources. April 10, 2003, House passed Wilson (NM) amendment to limit specified surface development to 2,000 acres (yeas 226, nays 202; Roll Call #134) and defeated Markey-Johnson (CT) amendment to strike Title IV, Division C (yeas 197, nays 228; Roll Call #135). Passed House April 11, 2003 (yeas 247, nays 175; Roll Call #145). Passed Senate (amended, no ANWR development provisions) July 31, 2003 (yeas 84, nays 15; Roll Call #317). Conference report (H.Rept. 108-375) filed November 18, 2003. Conference report agreed to in House November 18, 2003 (yeas 246, nays 180; Roll Call #630). Cloture motion failed in Senate November 21, 2003 (yeas 57, nays 40; Roll Call #456).

H.R. 39 (D. Young)

To repeal current prohibition against development in ANWR; and for other purposes. Introduced January 7, 2003; referred to Committee on Resources.

H.R. 770 (Markey)

To designate the 1002 area of ANWR as wilderness. Introduced February 13, 2003; referred to Committee on Resources.

H.R. 4514 (Pombo)

Virtually identical to House-passed version of H.R. 6; (see "Revenue Disposition" above, for only difference). Introduced June 4, 2004; referred to Committee on Resources.

S. 543 (Lieberman)

To designate the 1002 area of ANWR as wilderness. Introduced March 5, 2003; referred to Committee on Environment and Public Works.

SELECTED LEGISLATION IN THE 109TH CONGRESS

P.L. 109-58 (H.R. 6, Barton)

An omnibus energy act; Title XXII to open ANWR coastal plain to energy development. Introduced April 18, 2005; considered and marked up by Committee on Resources April 13, 2005 (no report). Considered by House April 20-21, 2005. Markey/Johnson amendment (H.Amdt. 73) to strike ANWR title rejected (yeas 200, nays 231, Roll Call #122) April 20. Passed April 21, 2005 (yeas 249, nays 183, Roll Call #132). Passed Senate, with no ANWR development provision, June 28, 2005 (yeas 85, nays 12, Roll Call #158). Conference agreement omitted ANWR title; signed by President, August 8, 2005.

P.L. 109-148 (H.R. 2863)

Provided for Defense appropriations. Conference report (H.Rept. 109-359) filed December 18, 2005 (Division C & D provided for ANWR development and revenue disposition). Cloture motion on filibuster on ANWR provision failed December 21, 2005 (yeas 56, nays 44, Roll Call #364). S.Con.Res. 74 corrected enrollment of the bill to delete Divisions C and D. Passed Senate December 21, 2005 (yeas 48, nays 45, Roll Call #365). Passed House December 22, 2005 on voice vote. Signed by President, December 30, 2005.

P.L. 109-171 (S. 1932)

Omnibus budget reconciliation; Title IV to provide for ANWR development. Introduced, referred to Committee on Budget, and reported October 27, 2005 (no written report). Passed Senate November 3, 2005 (yeas 52, nays 47, Roll Call #303). Passed House (amended) November 18, 2005. (For House action, see also H.R. 4241.) Title IV dropped in conference. House approved conference report (H.Rept. 109-362; yeas 212, nays 206, Roll Call #670). Senate approved report with an amendment (yeas 51, nays 50, Roll Call #363), December 21, 2005. House agreed to Senate amendment (yeas 216, nays 214, Roll Call #4), February 1, 2006. Signed by President, February 8, 2006.

H.Con.Res. 95 (Nussle)

FY2006 budget resolution, included spending targets for Committee on Resources. Introduced, referred to Committee on Budget, and reported March 11, 2005 (H.Rept. 109-17). Passed House March 17, 2005 (yeas 218, nays 214, Roll Call #88). Passed (amended) Senate in lieu of S.Con.Res. 18 (no report). April 28, 2005, House approved conference report (H.Rept. 109-62; yeas 214, nays 211, Roll Call #149), and Senate approved conference report (yeas 52, nays 47, Roll Call #114).

H.Con.Res. 376 (Nussle)

FY2007 budget resolution, to set spending targets including those for Committee on Resources. Introduced, referred to Committee on Budget, and reported March 31, 2006 (H.Rept. 109-402). Passed House May 18, 2006 (yeas 218, nays 210, Roll Call #158).

H.R. 39 (D. Young)

To repeal current prohibition against ANWR leasing; direct Secretary to establish competitive oil and gas leasing program; specify that the 1987 FLEIS is sufficient for compliance with the National Environmental Policy Act; authorize setasides up to 45,000 acres of Special Areas that restrict surface occupancy; set minimum for royalty payments and for tract sizes; and for other purposes. Introduced January 4, 2005; referred to Committee on Resources.

H.R. 567 (Markey)

To designate Arctic coastal plain of ANWR as wilderness. Introduced February 2, 2005; referred to Committee on Resources.

H.R. 4241 (Nussle)

FY2006 budget reconciliation. Title to open ANWR struck before floor consideration. Introduced November 7, 2005; passed House November 18, 2005 (yeas 217, nays 215, Roll Call #601). Inserted in lieu of the text of S. 1932.

H.R. 5429 (Pombo)

To create a leasing program to open ANWR to energy development. Introduced May 19, 2006; referred to Committee on Resources; passed House May 25, 2006 (yeas 225, nays 201, Roll Call #209).

S.Con.Res. 18 (Gregg)

FY2006 budget resolution; to set spending targets including those for Committee on Energy and Natural Resources. Introduced January 31, 2005; referred to Committee on Budget. Reported March 10, 2005 (no written report). Cantwell amendment (S.Amdt. 168, relating to ANWR) defeated March 16, 2005 (yeas 49, nays 51, Roll Call #52). Passed Senate March 17, 2005 (yeas 51, nays 49, Roll Call #81). Senate incorporated measure in

H.Con.Res. 95 as an amendment; passed H.Con.Res. 95 in lieu.

S.Con.Res. 74 (Cantwell)

Corrected enrollment of the bill H.R. 2863 (P.L. 109-148) to delete Divisions C and D. Passed Senate December 21, 2005 (yeas 48, nays 45, Roll Call #365). Passed House December 22, 2005, on voice vote.

S.Con.Res. 83 (Gregg)

FY2007 budget resolution; providing direction for cuts in mandatory spending targets only for Committee on Energy and Natural Resources. Introduced and reported by Committee on Budget on March 10, 2006 (no written report). Passed Senate March 16, 2006 (yeas 51, nays 49, Roll Call #74).

S. 261 (Lieberman)

To designate Arctic coastal plain of ANWR as wilderness. Introduced February 2, 2005; referred to Committee on Environment and Public Works.

S. 1891 (Murkowski)

To authorize energy development and economically feasible oil transportation in ANWR. Introduced October 19, 2005; referred to Committee on Energy and Natural Resources.

FOR ADDITIONAL READING

CRS Reports

CRS Report RL33872. *Arctic National Wildlife Refuge (ANWR): New Directions in the 110th Congress*, by M. Lynne Corn, Bernard A. Gelb, and Pamela Baldwin.

CRS Report RS22304. *ANWR and FY2006 Budget Reconciliation Legislation*, by Bill Heniff Jr. and M. Lynne Corn.

CRS Report RS21030. *ANWR Development: Economic Impacts*, by Bernard A. Gelb.

CRS Report RS22428. *ANWR Leasing Revenue Estimates*, by Bernard Gelb.

CRS Report RS21170. *ANWR Oil: Native Lands and State Waters*, by Bernard A. Gelb.

CRS Report RL31278. *Arctic National Wildlife Refuge: Background and Issues*, by M. Lynne Corn (Coordinator).

CRS Report RL33523. *Arctic National Wildlife Refuge (ANWR): Controversies for the 109th Congress*, by M. Lynne Corn, Bernard A. Gelb, and Pamela Baldwin.

CRS Report RL31022. *Arctic Petroleum Technology Developments*, by Bernard A. Gelb, M. Lynne Corn, and Terry R. Twyman.

CRS Report 98-814. *Budget Reconciliation Legislation: Development and Consideration*, by Bill Heniff Jr.

CRS Report RL30862. *The Budget Reconciliation Process: The Senate's "Byrd Rule,"* by Robert Keith.

CRS Report 98-815. *Budget Resolution Enforcement*, by Bill Heniff Jr.

CRS Report RL31033. *Energy Efficiency and Renewable Energy Fuel Equivalents to Potential Oil Production from the Arctic National Wildlife Refuge (ANWR)*, by Fred Sissine.

CRS Report RL31115. *Legal Issues Related to Proposed Drilling for Oil and Gas in the Arctic National Wildlife Refuge*, by Pamela Baldwin.

CRS Report RS22326. *Legislative Maps of ANWR*, by M. Lynne Corn, Pamela Baldwin.

CRS Report RL32108. *North Slope Infrastructure and the ANWR Debate*, by M. Lynne Corn.

CRS Report RS22143. *Oil and Gas Leasing in the Arctic National Wildlife Refuge (ANWR): The 2,000 Acre Limit*, by Pamela Baldwin and M. Lynne Corn.

CRS Report RS20368. *Overview of the Congressional Budget Process*, by Bill Heniff Jr.

CRS Report RS20602. *Presidential Authority to Create a National Monument on the Coastal Plain of the Arctic National Wildlife Refuge, and Possible Effects of Designation*, by Pamela Baldwin.

CRS Report RL31447. *Wilderness: Overview and Statistics*, by Ross W. Gorte.

Other Reports

National Academies of Science. *Cumulative Environmental Effects of Oil and Gas Activities on Alaska's North Slope.* March 2003. 452p. [http://www.nas.edu/].

Nelleman, C. and R. D. Cameron. "Cumulative Impacts of an Evolving Oilfield Complex on the Distribution of Calving Caribou." *Canadian Journal of Zoology*, 1998, Vol. 76, p. 1425.

U.S. Department of the Interior. Bureau of Land Management. *Overview of the 1991 Arctic National Wildlife Refuge Recoverable Petroleum Resource Update.* Washington, DC, April 8, 1991. 8 p., 2 maps.

U.S. Department of the Interior. Fish and Wildlife Service, Geological Survey, and Bureau of Land Management. *Arctic National Wildlife Refuge, Alaska, Coastal Plain Resource Assessment.* Report and Recommendation to the Congress of the United States and Final Legislative Environmental Impact Statement. Washington, DC, 1987. 208 p.

U.S. Department of the Interior. Geological Survey. *The Oil and Gas Resource Potential of the Arctic National Wildlife Refuge 1002 Area, Alaska.* 1999. 2 CD set. USGS Open File Report 98-34.

U.S. Department of the Interior. Geological Survey. *Arctic Refuge Coastal Plain Terrestrial Wildlife Research Summaries.* Biological Science Report USGS/BRD/BSR-2002-0001.

U.S. Department of the Interior. Geological Survey. "Evaluation of additional potential development scenarios for the 1002 Area of the Arctic National Wildlife Refuge." Memorandum from Brad Griffith, Assistant Leader, Alaska Cooperative Fish and Wildlife Research Unit, to Charles D. Groat, Director, U.S. Geological Survey. April 4, 2002.

U.S. Department of the Interior. Geological Survey. *Economics of 1998 U.S. Geological Survey's 1002 Area Regional Assessment: An Economic Update.* USGS Open File Report 2005-1359. Washington, DC, 2005.

U.S. General Accounting Office.23 *Arctic National Wildlife Refuge: An Assessment of Interior's Estimate of an Economically Viable Oil Field.* Washington, DC, July 1993. 31 p. GAO/RCED-93-130.

END NOTES

[1] This website and the others listed in this paragraph were last visited on March 30, 2007.

[2] Additional land was added in later years, bringing the current total to 19.3 million acres. Portions of the Refuge added in 1980 and later were not included in the wilderness system.

[3] For more on wilderness designation, see CRS Report RL31447, *Wilderness: Overview and Statistics*, by Ross W. Gorte.

[4] This report will use "Coastal Plain" to refer to the land legally designated under ANILCA and under subsequent Executive Branch rulings. In lower case ("coastal plain"), the term will be used in the geographic sense, i.e., the area north of the foothills of the Brooks Range. It stretches from the Canadian border west to Bering Straight. Its width varies from about 10 miles (at the Canadian border) to over 100 miles south of Barrow.

[5] For more history of legislation on ANWR and related developments, see CRS Report RL31278, *Arctic National Wildlife Refuge: Background and Issues*, coordinated by M. Lynne Corn and CRS Report RL31115, *Legal Issues Related to Proposed Drilling for Oil and Gas in the Arctic National Wildlife Refuge*, by Pamela Baldwin.

[6] Tom Doggett "Interview — Norton wants energy bill veto if no ANWR drilling," Reuters News Service (Sept. 19, 2002).

[7] Reconciliation bills in the Senate are considered under special rules that do not permit filibusters. See CRS Report 98-814, *Budget Reconciliation Legislation: Development and Consideration*, by Bill Heniff Jr. and CRS Report RL30862, *Budget Reconciliation Procedures: The Senate's 'Byrd Rule'*, by Robert Keith.

[8] See CRS Report RS20368, *Overview of the Congressional Budget Process*, by Bill Heniff Jr.

[9] For more on the budget process and budget enforcement, see CRS Report RS20368, *Overview of the Congressional Budget Process* and CRS Report 98-815, *Budget Resolution Enforcement*, by Bill Heniff Jr. For more on ANWR and reconciliation, see CRS Report RS22304, *ANWR and FY2006 Budget Reconciliation Legislation*, by Bill Heniff Jr. and M. Lynne Corn.

[10] See CRS Report RL30862, *The Budget Reconciliation Process: The Senate's 'Byrd Rule'*, by Robert Keith.

[11] For more background on each topic, see CRS Report RL31278, *Arctic National Wildlife Refuge: Background and Issues*, coordinated by M. Lynne Corn.

[12] See CRS Report RL32108, *North Slope Infrastructure and the ANWR Debate*, by M. Lynne Corn.

[13] For a discussion of an acreage limit, see CRS Report RS22143, *Oil and Gas Leasing in the Arctic National Wildlife Refuge (ANWR): The 2,000-Acre Limit*, by Pamela Baldwin and M. Lynne Corn.

[14] For more information, see CRS Report RL31115, *Legal Issues Related to Proposed Drilling for Oil and Gas in the Arctic National Wildlife Refuge (ANWR)*, by Pamela Baldwin (hereafter cited as CRS Report RL31115).

[15] For additional legal analysis, see CRS Report RL31115.

[16] See CRS Report RS22326, *Legislative Maps of ANWR*, by M. Lynne Corn and Pamela Baldwin.

[17] See CRS Report RL31115.

[18] The issue of new maps was first raised in legislation in the 109th Congress.

[19] See Figure 1 in CRS Report RS22326, *Legislative Maps of ANWR*, by M. Lynne Corn and Pamela Baldwin.

[20] For additional information on this issue, see CRS Report RL31115.

[21] See CRS Report RL33716, *Alaska Natural Gas Pipelines: Interaction of the Natural Gas and Steel Markets*, by Stephen Cooney and Robert Pirog.

[22] The Energy Policy and Conservation Act of 1975 (P.L. 94-163), the 1977 amendments to the Export Administration Act (P.L. 95-52 and P.L. 95-223), and the Export Administration Act of 1979 (P.L. 96-72), which replaced the Export Administration Act of 1969.

[23] This agency is now called the Government Accountability Office.

In: Arctic Natural Resources
Editor: Brian D. Raney

ISBN: 978-1-60692-131-9
© 2009 Nova Science Publishers, Inc.

Chapter 2

OIL AND GAS LEASING IN THE ARCTIC NATIONAL WILDLIFE REFUGE (ANWR): THE 2,000-ACRE LIMIT

Pamela Baldwin[1] and M. Lynne Corn[2]

SUMMARY

Congress is again considering whether to permit drilling for oil and gas on the coastal plain of the Arctic National Wildlife Refuge (ANWR), Alaska, or to maintain the current statutory prohibition on oil and gas development in the Refuge. The 109th Congress has considered the issue in authorizing bills, budget reconciliation bills, and an appropriation bill, but legislation opening the Refuge has not yet passed both chambers. Several measures would have limited the surface area that could be covered by certain oil production and support facilities to 2,000 acres of the 1.5 million acres of the Coastal Plain. These provisions raise several issues: they may not apply to some or all of the nearly 100,000 acres held by Native Americans in the Refuge that could be developed if the federal lands are opened to oil and gas development; and exactly what facilities would be subject to the limitation is not clear, although the limitation could constrain development if oil and gas discoveries are

---

[1] Pamela Baldwin, Legislative Attorney, American Law Division
[2] M. Lynne Corn, Specialist in Natural Resources, Resources, Science and Industry Division

widespread. This chapter discusses both legal and technical aspects of the 2,000-acre.

Congress is currently considering whether to permit drilling for oil and gas on the coastal plain of the Arctic National Wildlife Refuge (ANWR), Alaska. (Inaction would retain the current statutory prohibition on drilling in the Refuge.) Congress has considered the issue in authorizing bills, budget reconciliation bills — which cannot be filibustered in the Senate — and an appropriation bill.[1] The House-passed energy bill, H.R. 6, authorized leasing in ANWR, but the Senate did not pass a comparable bill, and the provisions were eliminated before enactment as P.L. 109-58. The Senate passed S. 1932, a budget reconciliation measure that would have authorized ANWR leasing, but the comparable House reconciliation measure did not, although an earlier version did. An attempt to add ANWR leasing to the Defense appropriations bill (H.R. 2863, P.L. 109-148) also failed.

Section 2207(a)(3) of H.R. 6 would have limited the amount of surface area that can be covered by oil production and support facilities to 2,000 acres of the 1.5 million acres of the Coastal Plain. Section 4001(f) of the Senate-passed S. 1932 contained a similar acreage limit, as did § 7(a)(3) of Div.C of H.R. 2863. The H.R. 6 provision would have directed the Secretary of the Interior to

> ensure that the maximum amount of surface acreage covered by production and support facilities, including airstrips and any areas covered by gravel berms or piers for support of pipelines, does not exceed 2,000 acres on the Coastal Plain.

Further, §2207(f) would have directed the Secretary to prepare periodic plans to avoid unnecessary duplication of facilities, and to encourage consolidation of facilities, among other things. This 2,000-acre "footprint" limitation is frequently cited as one way to minimize impacts of oil and gas development on the Refuge.[2] However, the H.R. 6 provision might not have limited exploratory facilities, and might not have limited some permanent structures. The acreage limit would have applied to some, and perhaps many, important development facilities. If facilities were limited as a result, or if oil and gas discoveries are widespread, some otherwise attractive discoveries could have been precluded, or the limitation might be lifted at a later date, to permit full development.

Section 2207(a) would have required the Secretary to administer the provisions of the title in a manner "consistent with the requirements of section

2203." Section 2203(a) required, among other things, that the Secretary ensure the receipt of fair market value by the public for the mineral resources to be leased.

There may have been a tradeoff between the direction to limit surface use for production and support facilities to 2,000 acres (as well as other constraints) and the determination of fair market value, since bidders could be expected to discount their bids or vary their bidding strategy to reflect the limitation.

The Senate measure, S. 1932, was less detailed than the House measure because it was a part of a budget reconciliation measure and special procedural rules applied, but leasing language in it and in the DOD appropriation bill was similar to that in H.R. 6. This chapter discusses both legal and technical aspects of the 2,000-acre limit.

Current Law on Development of ANWR

ANWR contains federal lands and nonfederal lands held by Native Americans. Section 1003 of the Alaska National Interest Lands Conservation Act (ANILCA)[3] prohibits oil and gas development in the Refuge unless Congress authorizes it. Under a 1983 Agreement (described below), if Congress repeals § 1003, and allows oil and gas development on the federal lands, development may also proceed on the Native American lands in the Refuge.[4]

Native American Lands in ANWR

The Alaska Native Claims Settlement Act (ANCSA)[5] resolved the claims of Alaska Natives against the United States, in part by establishing Native village corporations that could select surface land holdings, and Native regional corporations, associated with the village corporations, that could select primarily subsurface rights. The Kaktovik Inupiat Corporation (KIC) selected approximately three townships of lands in the *geographic* coastal plain of ANWR (a township is typically 23,040 acres). However, the legal boundaries of the *Coastal Plain*, as a term defined under ANILCA, were administratively drawn so as to exclude these three townships from the defined Coastal Plain. Also under ANILCA, KIC was entitled to select a fourth township, for a total of approximately 92,000 acres. This township is within the area administratively defined as the Coastal Plain.

In addition, there are several thousand acres of claimed or conveyed Native-owned *allotments* in the Refuge. These are basically surface ownerships, with the federal government reserving the oil, gas, and coal rights. Although allotments were originally restricted titles, under P.L. 108-337, allotments may now be subdivided and dedicated as if the surface estate were held in unrestricted, fee-simple title, a fact that could facilitate development on them if the Refuge is opened.

The Arctic Slope Regional Corporation (ASRC), the regional corporation associated with KIC, initially could not select lands within ANWR under the terms of ANCSA, but did receive the subsurface of these lands pursuant to a 1983 land exchange agreement, known as the *1983 Agreement* or the *Chandler Lake Agreement,* negotiated by then Secretary of the Interior James Watt. *ASRC lands* are defined in the agreement as including, as the context requires, the surface lands as well.[6] However, ASRC's oil and gas cannot be developed unless and until Congress authorizes oil and gas development on the federal lands in the Coastal Plain, on the ASRC lands, or both.

Appendices I and II of the 1983 Agreement contain terms and stipulations that would govern oil exploration activities on ASRC lands unless superseded by legislation or regulations. In addition, par. B.9 of Appendix II states that any oil and gas production activities *on ASRC lands* (which are both within and outside the Coastal Plain) shall be in accordance with the substantive statutory and regulatory requirements governing oil and gas exploration that are designed to protect the wildlife, habitat and environment of the coastal plain, ASRC lands, or both. Therefore, it appears that oil and gas production activities on ASRC lands would be subject to the same environmental requirements as those governing oil and gas production on federal lands.

Applicability of the 2,000-Acre Limit to Native Lands

The House-passed H.R. 6 did not address how the 2,000-acre limit might apply to oil and gas development on Native lands in ANWR, but the leasing regulations to be issued by the Secretary might. However, H.R. 6, applied to oil and gas activities in the *Coastal Plain* of ANWR, which was defined as the area identified on a map (now missing) referenced in ANILCA, and "as described in Appendix I to part 37 of title 50, Code of Federal Regulations." This CFR definition of the boundary of the Coastal Plain was published in 1983,[7] and excludes from the defined Coastal Plain the three townships then held by KIC. The description was not changed to reflect the fourth KIC township. Therefore, arguably three KIC townships are outside the defined Coastal Plain and one township is inside, with ASRC holdings underlying all of them. If the applicability of the 2,000-acre limitation to Native lands were to be litigated, a court might possibly find that (1) the provision is not "environmental protection" referred to in the 1983 Agreement, and therefore does not apply to development of any ASRC lands; (2) ASRC lands within the defined Coastal Plain (i.e., the fourth township lands) are subject to the 2,000-acre limit, but the others are not; or (3) all ASRC lands in the Refuge are bound by the restriction because of the wording of par. B.9 of Appendix II of the 1983 Agreement. The House-passed H.R. 6 did not address how the 2,000 acres would be allocated among ASRC and federal lessees if the acreage limit applies to ASRC lands. The Senate developed a new map of the Coastal Plain in connection with the Senate budget reconciliation measure. This map shows the Native lands as being within the Coastal Plain, but the bill does not clarify the intended applicability of leasing restrictions.

The limitation arguably would not apply to surface use of the three townships of KIC lands and allotments not in the defined Coastal Plain, and possibly not to those lands, wherever located, that are not being used as support for ASRC development. Therefore, it is possible that the 2,000-acre limit would not apply to some or all of the nearly 100,000 acres of Native lands that, under the 1983 Agreement, could be opened to oil and gas development in ANWR if the federal lands are.

Furthermore, the limitation might not apply to exploratory activities, which ASRC could conduct under the 1983 Agreement, which arguably is favorable to ASRC.[8]

Dispersion of Footprints

Technological advances have significantly reduced the size of oil drilling facilities in recent decades. However, assuming there were commercial finds, it is unlikely that full development of the Coastal Plain could be accomplished from a single compact site, and development could require a dispersed network of drill pads, roads, pipelines, gravel mines, and other structures. Even with advanced drilling techniques, there are limits to the lateral reach of drilling from a given wellhead. The current record in northern Alaska is 3.78 miles from one wellhead.[9] (The coastal plain is approximately 104 miles long and between 16 and 34 miles wide.) The extent of needed infrastructure (in both quantity and type) cannot be determined until or unless discoveries are actually made. Discoveries in the western part of the Refuge could necessitate fewer structures since some support or production structures might be located just outside of the Refuge's boundaries. Smaller, widely scattered fields would likely necessitate greater infrastructure than a few larger fields. Failure to find economic discoveries could lead to relatively minor, transient disturbance; important, scattered, or numerous finds could produce impacts lasting decades or possibly a century or more.

To What Facilities Does the Acreage Limitation Apply?

There is little consensus in the ANWR debate on what facilities and features might be considered to be part of development's footprint. The House-passed H.R. 6 required the Secretary to develop regulations, stipulations, and other implementation measures. The wording does not appear to include features some scientists, Natives, or environmentalists might wish: areas under elevated pipelines, or affected by blowing dust or visual impacts, etc. The potentially limited facilities can be divided into two categories: (1) areas directly covered with gravel (e.g., gravel roads, drill pads, airfields, culverts, bridges, ports, causeways, pump stations, water treatment facilities); and (2) areas whose surface is removed or covered (e.g., gravel mines, pipeline supports, water impoundments).

Airstrips and pipeline supports were expressly limited in §2007. But more debatable is the applicability of the limitation to other facilities: gravel mines, bridges, water impoundments, and causeways are examples. DOI's regulations that define the facilities to be limited would critically affect not only industry bids but also ultimately the potential for constraints on development.

As the Alpine model makes clear, new fields can make relatively small surface disturbance.[10] But as fields expand with new discoveries, surface disturbance increases. In the ANWR context, this means that an initial lease offering of 200,000 acres (the minimum required in H.R. 6) may not be seriously constrained by the wording of the 2,000-acre limit in §2207(a)(3), but scattered, numerous finds could reduce the remaining available acreage so as to constrain industry's participation in future lease sales. In this light, the Secretary's obligation to develop plans for consolidation of facilities would become both critical and more difficult, since the Secretary would need to allow for potential future discoveries.

Exploration in the ANWR Terrain

Exploration on the North Slope has typically been accomplished with ice roads and ice pads. But in the 1002 area, exploration may be more difficult than in previously developed areas. Liquid fresh water is much more scarce and the terrain more rolling in the Coastal Plain — conditions that elsewhere have resulted in the use of gravel roads for safety reasons.[11] Also, the warming trend of the last few decades has cut the season for ice construction from over 200 days to about half of its previous length.[12] In combination, these factors might necessitate permanent exploration facilities (e.g., roads, pads, and gravel mines) in ANWR, and if the 2,000 acre limit does not apply to exploration facilities, these facilities could be located throughout the Coastal Plain. If exploration is successful, facilities on specific leases might be converted to production facilities, raising the issue of whether such converted facilities would be limited once they are used in production.

Interaction of Acreage Limit and Economics

A company's investment calculus would affect the amount the company would bid for a lease — or its willingness to bid at all. A very large prospect, near existing development at the coast, close to gravel sources and the limited year-round liquid fresh water, would likely generate industry interest even under tight environmental restrictions. Large but widely scattered or less convenient prospects would present opportunities which could be profitable under some regulatory scenarios, but not others. And small, or otherwise unattractive prospects might not be of interest under any foreseeable conditions. A lessee will judge whether and how quickly to proceed[13] based on the size of the field, quality of the oil, expected prices, regulatory costs, and other considerations. This decision may be affected by limits on the operation of the field such as the size of the drill pads, access to fresh water, or limits on gravel roads (forcing expensive seasonal limitations and air transport for work crews). All else being equal, if restrictions (including acreage limitations) became more costly, fewer prospects might be developed.

If the footprints of production and support (and possibly exploration) facilities throughout the Coastal Plain were strictly limited to a total of 2,000 acres, a tradeoff could occur between this limit and the determination of fair market value for them, unless the facilities subject to limits were defined very narrowly or discoveries prove limited.

Responses to Acreage Limits

The acreage limitation will be closely watched both from the perspective of its putative contribution to limiting adverse environmental affects and its possible constraint on development. If development legislation is enacted, environmentalists will likely focus on a strict interpretation of the limit and on DOI's mandate in §2207(f) to consolidate and minimize the footprint. Development proponents will likely focus on its costs. Depending on how much oil is found, how it is distributed, and where the limit is applied, the effect of the 2,000-acre limit could range from being irrelevant to a significant factor affecting any development. In the latter case, industry's response could be expected to include technological improvements, a shift of facilities to uncontrolled areas, a changed bidding strategy, an effort to obtain regulatory or legislative relief, or a combination of these options.

END NOTES

[1] See CRS Issue Brief IB10136, *Arctic National Wildlife Refuge (ANWR): Controversies for the 109th Congress*, by Lynne M. Corn, Bernard A. Gelb, and Pamela Baldwin.

[2] Supporters of the limitation favor development, and argue that by limiting surface development, environmental impacts will be reduced. Opponents of ANWR development argue that what they see as major impacts (e.g., caribou displacement, dust, subsistence and recreation resources) would still occur, and an acreage limit would create a false sense of a safety net for the Refuge.

[3] P.L. 96-487, 94 Stat. 2374, 16 U.S.C. §§ 3101, *et seq.*

[4] For a more detailed discussion of legal issues related to the Native lands in ANWR, see CRS Report RL31115, *Legal Issues Related to Proposed Drilling for Oil and Gas in the Arctic National Wildlife Refuge (ANWR)*, by Pamela Baldwin.

[5] P.L. 92-203, 85 Stat. 688, 43 U.S.C. §§ 1601, *et seq.*

[6] An owner of a mineral estate typically also has the right to use as much of the surface as is reasonably necessary to develop the minerals.

[7] 48 *Fed. Reg.* 7936, 7980 (February 24, 1983).

[8] For example, if ASRC and the United States disagree as to the environmental impacts of ASRC's exploratory activities, the United States must get a court to agree with its restrictions.

[9] See CRS Report RL32108, *North Slope Infrastructure and the ANWR Debate*, by M. Lynne Corn, and see CRS Report RL31022, *Arctic Petroleum Technology Developments*, by Bernard A. Gelb et al.

[10] At Alpine, on 40,000 acres of state, Native, and federal land west of Prudhoe Bay, development initially consisted of about 100 acres of pads, a road, and an airstrip, plus a 150-acre gravel mine. Approved expansion will create five new drill pads and 28 miles of new gravel roads, making an additional 251 acres of roads, causeways, and other structures, plus a 65-acre gravel mine, for a total of 566 acres (p. 1036 in U.S. Dept. of the Interior, Bureau of Land Management, *Alpine Satellite Development Plan, Final Environmental Impact Statement*, Sept. 2004).

[11] State of Alaska, Dept. of Natural Resources, Div. of Oil and Gas, *Supplement to North Slope Areawide Best Interest Finding*, July 24, 2002, 3 pp.

[12] National Research Council, *Cumulative Effects of Oil and Gas Activities on Alaska's North Slope*, Mar. 2003, pp. 134-137 and figs. 7-8.

[13] For diligence requirements under the Mineral Leasing Act, see 30 U.S.C. §226(e) and (i).

In: Arctic Natural Resources
Editor: Brian D. Raney

Chapter 3

ENGINEERING AND ECONOMICS OF THE UNITED STATES GEOLOGICAL SURVEY CIRCUM-ARCTIC OIL AND GAS RESOURCE APPRAISAL (CARA) PROJECT

Mahendra K. Verma[1], Loring P. (Red) White[2] and Donald L. Gautier[3]

INTRODUCTION

This Open-File report contains illustrative materials, in the form of PowerPoint slides, used for an oral presentation given at the Fourth U.S. Geological Survey Workshop on Reserve Growth of petroleum resources held on March 10-11, 2008. The presentation focused on engineering and economic aspects of the Circum-Arctic Oil and Gas Resource Appraisal (CARA) project, with a special emphasis on the costs related to the development of hypothetical oil and gas fields of different sizes and reservoir characteristics in the North Danmarkshavn Basin off the northeast coast of Greenland.

The individual PowerPoint slides highlight the topics being addressed in an abbreviated format; they are discussed below, and are amplified with

[1] USGS, Central Region, P.O. Box 25046, MS 939, Denver, CO 80225
[2] USGS, 1321 Cortlandt Street, Houston, TX 77008
[3] USGS, Western Region, 345 Middlefield Road, Menlo Park, CA 94025

additional text as appropriate. Also included in this report are the summary results of a typical "run" to generate the necessary capital and operating costs for the development of an offshore oil field off the northeast coast of Greenland; the data are displayed in MS Excel format generated using Questor software (IHS Energy, Inc.).

U.S. Geological Survey (USGS) acknowledges that this report includes data supplied by IHS Energy, Inc.; Copyright (2008) all rights reserved. IHS Energy has granted USGS the permission to publish this report.

Content of Slides

Slide 1. – Overall objective of CARA project and the general approach to estimating resource development costs are presented.

Slide 2. – Additional engineering and economic considerations relative to estimating resource development costs are listed. Application of Questor (IHS Energy, Inc.), as an integral part of the resource development study is introduced. Questor generates the following three main parameters that are used to develop resource cost (unit curves) – production profile, capital expenditure (CAPEX), and operating expenditure (OPEX).

Slide 3. – It is pointed out that Questor is directly linked to a large IHS database, which is the source for all the geologic, reservoir, production, and cost data. It also emphasizes that, due to lack of cost data for the Arctic region, some of the costs in Questor's output need to be adjusted to adequately address the unique operating conditions and ice management concerns that impact resource development in the Arctic region. Following are few examples of cost adjustments, made in consultation with the technical group of IHS Energy, Inc.:

1. Drilling rig: (a) consider the option and added expense of using a 'fourth generation' drilling rig, (b) change the floating bare rig unit cost by 10 percent, (c) change the transportation cost by 10 percent, (d) increase the number of drilling days by 15 percent to allow for the extra expense of site preparation, (e) add logging days equal to the number of wells expected to be drilled, and (f) make the cost of Design and Project Management approximately equal to 10 percent of the total drilling cost.

2. Topsides (oil processing facility on top of floating vessel): increase the material cost by 25 percent.
3. Booster pumps: (a) install a pump capable of sustaining a flow of oil for approximately every 200 km or more as defined by the onshore oil booster pump scheme, (b) add the cost of cable at the rate of $100/m, (c) calculate the number of days for cable installation by dividing the length of the pipe in km by 4, and introduce the cable installation cost (possibly $200,000/day), and (d) make the Design and Project Management Cost equal to 10 percent of the total cost.
4. Ice management: use the 'special item' in the Field/Project cost under the 'Offshore' tab of the Total Operating Cost Summary for adding possibly as much as $500,000,000 per year.
5. Pipelines: (a) insulate all offshore pipes in water depths of more than 200 m, (b) bury pipes where water depths are less than 200 m to avoid scouring by ice berg, and (c) insulate onshore pipe.

Slide 4. – The main types of data needed for input to Questor are listed. Some of the data are readily available, such as reserve volume, reservoir depth, water depth, and distance to shore. Other parameters are calculated from engineering correlations, such as peak field production, gas-oil ratio equation, pressure gradient, and well productivity. In addition, Questor prompts the user to choose a procurement strategy whereby appropriate regions are selected for front-end engineering design (FEED); engineering, procurement, and construction (EPC); and associated cost data.

Slide 5. – A schematic diagram of essential facilities for the drilling, production processing, and transport of crude oil, specific to an offshore field is presented. Questor helps design field development that includes drilling rigs/equipment items; subsea well completion, oil production, and processing facilities (both offshore and offshore); pipelines to transfer the oil from offshore to an export terminal; and booster pumps. With respect to fields off the northeast coast of Greenland, oil processing and transport to market would include the following stages: (a) oil processing offshore with partial stabilization of oil, (b) oil transportation via pipelines to the onshore facility at Flade Budgt where oil is fully stabilized, (c) oil transportation via a subsea pipeline running along the coast to the oil Storage and Export Terminal located at Angmagssalik, and (d) oil tankers are used to transport oil from the Oil Storage and Export Terminal to the New York port for distribution.

Slide 6. – Use of Questor results to estimate resource development costs is described, and the five principal variables –recoverable hydrocarbon volume, well productivity, reservoir/drilling depth, water depth, and distance to shore – that affect the CAPEX and OPEX are listed. The need to apply these variables in a number of different "runs" is emphasized in order to develop statistical cost functions.

Slide 7. – The reports resulting from the use of Questor software are described, and a typical custom report is presented for one development scenario. The report includes, in tabular form, a Summary of all the input data, a Combined Investment and Production Profile, a Combined Cost (CAPEX) Summary and Total Operating Cost Summary.

The PowerPoint slides given below are followed by an Excel spreadsheet. This spreadsheet constitutes a custom report for one of the runs, giving the project summary and combined investment and production profiles, and investment and operating costs.

Study Objective

- The objective of the CARA project is to assess the Arctic region for its hydrocarbon resource volume and its development cost by integrating geologic, engineering and economic (cost) data.

  Geology defines the hydrocarbon volume of a resource.
  Engineering looks at the development strategy.
  Economics (or unit cost curves) defines the value of a resource development.

Engineering and Economics

- Hydrocarbon volume along with the following reservoir/engineering and cost data are required for the development of resource cost (unit) curves:

  Production ProfileCapital
  Expenditure (CAPEX)

Operating Expenditure (OPEX)

- Questor (IHS Inc.) is a tool that generates these above parameters for various field development scenarios.

Questor's Link to a Database and Policy Decisions for Better Estimates of Cost

- Questor has a direct link to a large database with geologic, reservoir, production and cost data from various countries/regions around the world.
- In consultation with IHS technical support group, certain costs in the Questor were added/increased to account for harsh operating conditions and ice management in the Arctic region.

Questor and its Input

The following parameters are required as an input to Questor:

- Reserve volume
- Reservoir depth
- Reservoir pressure
- Solution gas-oil ratio
- Water depth
- Fluid gravity
- Estimated ultimate recovery per well
- Average well productivity
- Distance to shore

A Schematic of the Facility Design for an Offshore Oil Field

How Questor Results are to be used to Develop Resource Cost Curves?

- Make a number of runs with Questorusing a range of values for each of the following variables:

  Reserve volume
  Well productivity
  Reservoir/drilling depth
  Water depth
  Distance to shore

- Use results from the runs to develop statistical cost functions.

Results from Questor

Questor allows printing of either detailed or custom reports.

- Detailed report: giving details of CAPEX and OPEX, and a report could be up to 100s of pages long.
- Custom report: giving Summary sheet, CAPEX and OPEX, making it easier for a review.

A typical custom report in Excel format is presented separately.

OFFSHORE PROJECT SUMMARY

Project name	NEG_MKV_OIL_RUN_27B
Country	North America Average
Region	North America
Basin	Arctic Ocean Region Average

Procurement strategy		Currency	Rate/$		Procurement strategy		Currency	Rate/$
Offshore	North Atlantic Ocean Regi	$	1.00		Onshore	North America Average	$	1.00
Contingency	N. North Sea (Norway)	NOK	5.78		Contingency	N. America	US$	1.00
Equipment	N. North Sea (Norway)	NOK	5.78		Equipment	Western Europe	US$	1.00
Materials	N. North Sea (Norway)	NOK	5.78		Materials	Western Europe	US$	1.00
Fabrication	S. E. Asia	US$	1.00		Prefabrication	Asia	US$	1.00
Linepipe	N. North Sea (Norway)	NOK	5.78		Linepipe	Eastern Europe	US$	1.00
Installation	N. North Sea (U.K.)	£	0.50		Construction	Western Europe	US$	1.00
Design & PM	N. North Sea (Norway)	NOK	5.78		Design & PM	Western Europe	US$	1.00
Opex	N. North Sea (Norway)	NOK	5.78		Certification	Western Europe	US$	1.00
Certification	N. North Sea (Norway)	NOK	5.78		Opex	Western Europe	US$	1.00
Freight	N. North Sea (U.K.)	£	0.50					

Technical database			Technical database	
Offshore	N. North Sea (Norway)		Onshore	N. America

Unit set	Oilfield
Development type	Oil
Development concept	Semi-submersible + Subsea tie-back

Overall input

Design oil production flowrate	220.00	Mbbl/day		Reserves	1000.00	MMbbl
Design associated gas flowrate	205.00	MMscf/day		Water depth	450.00	m
Water injection capacity factor	1.20			Reservoir depth	2950.00	m
Design water injection flowrate	264.00	Mbbl/day		Reservoir pressure	4120.00	psia
Design gas injection rate	205.00	MMscf/day		Reservoir length	14.10	km
Gas oil ratio	931.00	scf/bbl		Reservoir width	7.07	km
Design factor	1.10					

Fluid characteristics

Oil density @ STP	35.00	°API		H2S content	10.00	ppm
CO2 content	1.00	%		Gas molecular weight	30.10	

Production profile characteristics

Plateau rate	200.00	Mbbl/day		Years to plateau	3.00	year
Productivity	50.00	MMbbl/well		Plateau duration	7.00	year
Peak well flow	10.00	Mbbl/day		Field life	21.00	year
Maximum drilling stepout	3.00	km		Onstream days	350.00	day

Export methods

Oil export method	offshore loading		Gas export method	inject into reservoir	
Distance to delivery point	1.00	km	Distance to delivery point	0.00	km

Number of wells

Production wells	20		Gas injection wells	7
Water injection wells	8			

Field level miscellaneous data

Distance to operations base	120.00	km
Distance to delivery point	120.00	km
Maximum drilling stepout	3.00	km
Maximum ambient temperature	2.00	°C

COMBINED INVESTMENT AND PRODUCTION PROFILES

Project name: NEG_MKV_OIL_RUN_27B
Currency (millions $): US Dollars

		Cost/boe		
boe/bbl Oil	1			
boe/bbl Condensate	0.8	Capital cost	0.8	Cost/boe
boe/Mscf Gas	0.17		0.17	Cost/boe

			Cost/boe			
E & A cost	0				Capital cost	13,185.23 / 13.19
Cost/boe	0	Drilling cost	2,775.37 / 2.78		Operating cost	22,549.45 / 22.55
		Facilities cost	10,409.86 / 10.41			

Lifecycle cost	37,034.89	Cost/boe	37.03
Decommission cost	1,300.21	Cost/boe	1.3
Design production	77		71.69

Year	EXPLORATION & APPRAISAL				PROD. DRILLING		CAPITAL COSTS			OPERATING COSTS			DECOMM.	PRODUCTION		
	Seismic	Expl.	Well test	Apprsl	Tangible	Intangible	Facilities	Pipelines	Other facilities	Fixed OPEX	Tariffs	Mods	Abandnmt	Oil MMbbl/yr	Cond. MMbbl/yr	Gas Bscf/yr
TOTAL	0.00	0.00	0.00	0.00	384.97	2,390.40	3,236.89	6,864.42	308.55	20,473.31	2,076.14	0.00	1,300.21	1,000.00	0.00	0.00
1					11.94	82.01	296.63	1,092.81								
2					45.41	77.32	528.95	3,524.86								
3					74.47	192.70	531.73	870.82								
4					78.28	387.07	1,448.42	543.72	79.95							
5					78.28	592.95	197.92	566.38	187.89							
6					66.35	592.95	233.24	285.83	40.71							
7					28.97	367.81										
8					1.27	97.59				880.32	36.33			17.50		
9										881.94	72.66			35.00		
10										883.55	109.00			52.50		
11										1,099.71	145.33			70.00		
12										885.36	145.33			70.00		
13										910.01	145.33			70.00		
14										885.17	145.33			70.00		
15										1,198.49	145.33			70.00		
16										885.17	145.33			70.00		
17										1,472.91	145.33			70.00		
18										909.60	136.10			65.55		
19										1,098.55	119.19			57.41		
20										883.36	104.38			50.28		
21										882.77	91.41			44.03		
22										882.45	80.05			38.56		
23										1,219.99	70.11			33.77		
24										881.43	61.39			29.57		
25										881.09	53.77			25.90		
26										880.80	47.09			22.68		
27										1,090.33	41.24			19.86		
28										880.31	36.11		1,300.21	17.39		
29																

COMBINED COST SUMMARY

Project	NEO_MKV_OIL_RUN_27B
Location	North America
Development type	OK

Sub total	11,339,191,000
Contingency	1,846,024,000
Grand total	13,185,215,000

Currency	US Dollars

Procurement strategy: Offshore	North Atlantic Ocean Region
Procurement strategy: Onshore	North America Average

Cost centre	Grand total	Equipment	Materials	Fabrication	Prefabrication	Installation/Construction	H.U. & C	Design	Project management	Ins. & cert.	Contingency
Topsides 1	576,644,000	162,995,000	76,183,000	52,315,000		0	16,236,000	153,737,000	38,139,000	24,983,000	52,432,000
Semi-sub 1	786,599,000	562,413,000	19,826,000	2,862,000		8,632,000	4,620,000	12,882,000	12,720,000	31,214,000	131,160,000
Offshore pipeline 2	37,561,000		2,778,000			26,017,000		618,000	1,696,000		4,899,000
Offshore pipeline 1	412,162,000		185,611,000			134,190,000		5,877,000	15,858,000	17,666,000	53,790,000
Offshore pipeline 3	6,495,489,000		3,392,620,000			1,783,348,000		47,173,000	131,616,000	285,238,000	835,489,000
Offshore loading 1	340,752,000	172,963,000	16,805,000			17,330,000		17,160,000	48,040,000	13,522,000	56,792,000
Offshore drilling 1	1,433,580,000	94,758,000	62,142,000			837,422,000		50,160,000	83,280,000	56,888,000	208,930,000
Offshore drilling 2	1,341,786,000	90,046,000	58,583,000			780,660,000		47,424,000	88,192,000	53,245,000	223,630,000
Subsea 1	276,260,000	73,178,000	32,392,000			95,485,000		11,924,000	6,276,000	18,960,000	46,043,000
Subsea 2	270,186,000	86,424,000	28,363,000			90,663,000		12,472,000	6,572,000	16,721,000	45,031,000
Subsea Booster P.S.	38,569,000	24,051,000	1,395,000	7,000		4,028,000		1,368,000	2,544,000	1,670,000	3,506,000
Subsea Booster P.S.	38,569,000	24,051,000	1,395,000	7,000		4,028,000		1,368,000	2,544,000	1,670,000	3,506,000
Subsea Booster P.S.	38,569,000	24,051,000	1,395,000	7,000		4,028,000		1,368,000	2,544,000	1,670,000	3,506,000
Subsea Booster P.S.	38,569,000	24,051,000	1,395,000	7,000		4,028,000		1,368,000	2,544,000	1,670,000	3,506,000
Subsea Booster P.S.	38,569,000	24,051,000	1,395,000	7,000		4,028,000		1,368,000	2,544,000	1,670,000	3,506,000
Subsea Booster P.S.	38,569,000	24,051,000	1,395,000	7,000		4,028,000		1,368,000	2,544,000	1,670,000	3,506,000
Subsea Booster P.S.	38,569,000	24,051,000	1,395,000	7,000		4,028,000		1,368,000	2,544,000	1,670,000	3,506,000
Subsea Booster P.S.	38,569,000	24,051,000	1,395,000	7,000		4,028,000		1,368,000	2,544,000	1,670,000	3,506,000
Offshore Prod. Fac.	238,798,000	36,882,000	28,523,000		12,264,000	86,617,000		25,200,000	13,872,000	4,272,000	31,148,000
Storage and Export 1	516,633,000	35,727,000	59,074,000		13,222,000	235,280,000		85,694,000	36,240,000	8,809,000	67,367,000
Onshore pipeline 1	3,071,000		1,001,000			1,084,000		245,000	288,000	52,000	491,000
Onshore pipeline 3	3,071,000		1,001,000			1,084,000		245,000	396,000	52,000	491,000
Onshore pipeline 2	3,071,000		1,001,000			1,084,000		245,000	288,000	52,000	491,000
Infra- Onshore Fac.	115,903,000	86,506,000	86,505,000					6,314,000	6,648,000	1,969,000	15,096,000
Infra- Terminal	115,903,000	86,506,000	86,505,000					6,314,000	6,648,000	1,969,000	15,096,000
TOTALS	13,185,215,000	1,487,064,000	4,190,075,000	55,363,000	25,506,000	4,086,461,000	28,850,860	472,556,000	525,696,000	515,710,000	1,846,024,000

Total operating cost summary

		Totals	Year 1	Year 2	Year 3	Year 4	Year 5	Year 6	Year 7	Year 8	Year 9	Year 10	Year 11	Year 12	Year 13	Year 14	Year 15	Year 16	Year 17	Year 18	Year 19	Year 20	Year 21
Grand total operating cost	$	22,548,433,900	916,653,900	894,952,900	982,992,900	1,046,943,300	1,030,984,300	1,065,336,300	1,055,460,900	1,345,819,900	1,030,699,900	1,816,238,600	1,945,790,900	1,217,778,900	982,773,900	974,161,990	962,933,990	1,260,989,990	942,828,990	904,843,990	907,868,990	1,151,989,990	875,482,990
Direct costs																							
Operating personnel costs	$	1,566,645,900	71,745,000	71,745,000	71,745,000	71,745,000	71,745,000	71,745,000	71,745,000	71,745,000	71,745,000	71,745,000	71,745,000	71,745,000	71,745,000	71,745,000	71,745,000	71,745,000	71,745,000	71,745,000	71,745,000	71,745,000	71,745,000
Inspection & maintenance costs	$	2,877,503,900	152,295,000	152,295,000	112,295,000	115,782,000	112,228,000	131,102,000	112,295,000	115,791,000	112,295,000	964,215,000	121,103,000	115,791,000	112,295,000	112,295,000	152,229,000	152,816,000	112,295,000	112,295,000	112,295,000	112,295,000	112,295,000
Logistics & consumables costs	$	477,695,900	20,295,000	21,716,000	25,146,000	24,577,000	24,373,000	24,373,000	24,377,000	24,577,000	24,377,000	24,577,000	24,377,000	24,577,000	22,296,000	22,498,000	22,598,000	24,378,000	24,278,000	24,877,000	24,711,000	26,715,000	26,276,000
Well costs	$	908,837,900	0	0	0	961,376,000	0	0	0	227,860,000	0	0	0	181,970,000	0	0	0	215,980,000	0	0	0	981,373,000	0
Insurance costs	$	1,302,446,900	62,069,000	62,069,000	62,060,000	62,069,000	62,069,000	62,069,000	62,069,000	62,069,000	62,069,000	62,069,000	62,069,000	62,069,000	62,069,000	62,069,000	62,069,000	62,069,000	62,069,000	62,069,000	62,069,000	62,069,000	62,069,000
Direct costs total	$	7,196,275,900	298,104,000	307,383,000	269,017,000	435,486,000	276,914,000	309,409,000	275,148,000	511,461,000	265,448,000	722,806,000	285,919,000	434,415,000	268,003,000	268,319,000	298,510,000	540,667,000	265,345,000	266,345,000	423,724,000	421,375,000	265,145,000
Field project costs	$	13,348,011,900	614,167,000	614,333,000	614,338,000	664,234,000	614,161,000	626,406,000	654,284,000	667,298,000	634,734,000	759,202,000	896,150,000	664,350,000	614,448,000	614,445,000	614,407,000	608,237,000	614,223,000	614,276,000	614,276,000	650,894,000	614,166,000
Tariff costs	$	2,876,123,900	56,632,000	72,664,000	108,867,000	145,825,000	145,926,000	145,909,000	145,928,000	145,928,000	145,921,000	146,225,000	756,932,000	175,188,000	184,380,000	93,410,000	469,652,000	71,165,000	83,964,000	63,766,000	63,865,000	61,296,000	36,117,000

In: Arctic Natural Resources
Editor: Brian D. Raney

ISBN: 978-1-60692-131-9
© 2009 Nova Science Publishers, Inc.

Chapter 4

ASSESSMENT OF UNDISCOVERED PETROLEUM RESOURCES OF THE NORTH AND EAST MARGINS OF THE SIBERIAN CRATON, RUSSIAN FEDERATION

United States Geological Survey

Four geologic provinces located along the north and east margins of the Siberian craton were assessed for undiscovered crude oil, natural gas, and natural gas liquids/condensates resources as part of the U.S. Geological Survey's (USGS) Circum-Arctic Oil and Gas Resource Appraisal. Using a geology-based methodology, the USGS estimated the mean undiscovered, conventional petroleum resources in these provinces to be approximately 28 billion barrels of oil equivalent, including approximately 8 billion barrels of crude oil, 106 trillion cubic feet of natural gas, and 3 billion barrels of natural gas liquids.

INTRODUCTION

In 2007, the U.S. Geological Survey (USGS) completed an assessment of potential undiscovered, technically recoverable (assuming the absence of sea ice) crude oil, natural gas, and natural gas liquids (collectively referred to as petroleum) resources in the Yenisey-Khatanga Basin, Lena-Anabar Basin,

Lena-Vilyui Basin (northern part), and the Zyryanka Basin Provinces of the Russian Federation (Figure 1). As with other areas and basins assessed in the USGS Circum-Arctic Oil and Gas Resource Appraisal (CARA) program, this area shares important characteristics with many Arctic basins, including sparse data, significant petroleum-resource potential, geologic uncertainty, and technical barriers that impede exploration and development. As defined for CARA, the Yenisey-Khatanga Basin Province includes approximately 391,000 km^2; the Lena-Anabar Basin Province, approximately 125,000 km^2; the northern Priverkhoyansk part of the Lena-Vilyuy Basin Province, approximately 55,000 km^2, and the Zyryanka Basin Province, approximately 56,000 km^2.

ASSESSMENT UNITS

The Yenisey-Khatanga Basin, Lena-Anabar Basin, and Lena-Vilyui Basin Provinces formed on the margins of the Siberian craton and later underwent compressional deformation as a result of collision with other tectonic plates. The sedimentary successions of these provinces are similar because of their close proximity (Figure 1) and similar depositional histories. The Zyryanka Basin is a foreland basin that developed on top of a backarc basin formed during accretion and deformation of neighboring tectonic plates. This basin is bounded by extensively deformed rocks derived from oceanic/island arc terranes that, in part, were subjected to Cenozoic extension.

For purposes of assessment, the four provinces were subdivided into seven geologically distinctive assessment units (AUs) on the basis of structural style—the Khatanga Saddle, Yenisey-Khatanga Basin, Lena-Anabar Basin, Lena-Anabar Updip, Sukhan-Motorchun Riphean Rift, Northern Priverkhoyansk Foredeep, and Zyryanka Basin AUs (Figure 1). The Lena-Anabar Basin AU was evaluated using two mutually exclusive geological scenarios (table 1); the differences between them are such that the populations of undiscovered accumulations cannot be statistically combined into a single distribution. One scenario assumes that a thick lower Paleozoic section was deposited and subsequently removed by erosion before the Permian. This scenario allows for the possibility of Precambrian and Cambrian source rocks to have become thermally mature with respect to petroleum generation during the Paleozoic, and thus any accumulated petroleum would have been destroyed by the subsequent erosion. The other scenario assumes no early

Paleozoic deposition and petroleum maturation probably occurred during the late Paleozoic and early Mesozoic. All of the AUs were quantitatively assessed.

PETROLEUM SYSTEM ELEMENTS

Two total petroleum systems were defined in each of the Yenisey-Khatanga Basin, Lena-Anabar Basin, and Lena-Vilyui Basin Provinces—one with Proterozoic and Cambrian source rocks and the other with upper Paleozoic through Jurassic source rocks. However, because of suspected mixing of petroleum, the two systems were combined into the Proterozoic-Paleozoic-Mesozoic Composite Total Petroleum System (TPS) for these provinces. In addition, a Mesozoic Composite TPS was defined within the Yenisey-Khatanga Basin Province to exclude Proterozoic and Paleozoic rocks with low petroleumsource potential. A Paleozoic-Mesozoic Composite TPS was identified in the Zyryanka Basin Province. This TPS, which incorporates the Zyryanka Basin AU (table 1), contains sedimentary rocks that are different from those in the other provinces. The greatest geologic uncertainty for the assessment of all AUs is with respect to the timing of petroleum charge and preservation of accumulations.

Analyses of crude oil and natural gas from producing wells, shows, seeps, and bitumen indicate the presence of mature source rocks in all of the AUs. Major reservoir rocks include Proterozoic and lower Paleozoic carbonate and clastic rocks and upper Paleozoic and Mesozoic clastic rocks. Postulated traps for petroleum accumulations include compressional structures (folds and thrust faults) and updip pinchouts, as well as other stratigraphic traps.

RESOURCE SUMMARY

The USGS assessed undiscovered conventional, technically recoverable petroleum resources (discovered reserves not included), resulting in the estimated mean volumes of a probability distribution of approximately 8 billion barrels (1 billion metric tons) of crude oil, 106 trillion cubic feet (3 trillion cubic meters) of natural gas, and 3 billion barrels (400 million metric tons) of natural gas liquids (table 1). The largest volume of undiscovered petroleum is estimated to be in the Yenisey-Khatanga Basin AU.

REFERENCE

IHS Energy, 2006, International petroleum exploration and production database [includes data current through December, 2006]: IHS Energy; database available from IHS Energy, 15 Inverness Way East, Englewood, CO 80112, U.S.A.

CIRCUM-ARCTIC PETROLEUM RESOURCE ASSESSMENT TEAM

T.R. Klett (assessing geologist), K.J. Bird, P.J. Brown II, R.R. Charpentier, D.L. Gautier, D.W. Houseknecht, T.E. Moore, J.K. Pitman, R.W. Saltus, C.J. Schenk, A.K. Shah, K.I. Takahashi, M.E. Tennyson, and C.J. Wandrey

ACKNOWLEDGMENT

Geographical Information System analysis was performed by F.M. Persits.

Table 1. Assessment results of geologic provinces along the north and east margins of the Siberian craton(conventional undiscovered resources).

Total Petroleum Systems and Assessment Units	AU Probability	Field Type	Oil (MMB)				Total Undiscovered Resources Gas (BCF)				NGL (MMB)			
			F95	F50	F5	Mean	F95	F50	F5	Mean	F95	F50	F5	Mean
YENISEY-KHATANGA BASIN PROVINCE (1175)														
Proterozoic-Paleozoic-Mesozoic Composite TPS (117501)														
Khatanga Saddle AU (11750101)	0.500	Oil	0	0	1,376	327	0	0	932	206	0	0	25	6
		Gas					0	0	6,764	1,797	0	0	182	48
Mesozoic Composite TPS (117502)														
Yenisey-Khatanga Basin AU (11750201)	1.000	Oil	2,200	4,847	9,716	5,257	11,604	26,571	55,375	29,078	305	710	1,528	786
		Gas					38,629	66,089	108,413	68,884	1,009	1,754	2,929	1,835
Total undiscovered petroleum resources, Province 1175						5,584				99,965				2,675
LENA-ANABAR BASIN PROVINCE (1200)														
Proterozoic-Paleozoic-Mesozoic Composite TPS (120001)														
Lena-Anabar Basin AU (12000101) Scenario 1, 90% probability	0.480	Oil	0	0	7,451	2,074	0	0	6,174	1,628	0	0	169	44
		Gas					0	0	2,693	654	0	0	73	17
Lena-Anabar Basin AU (12000101) Scenario 2, 10% probability	0.320	Oil	0	0	2,611	526	0	0	2,143	416	0	0	58	11
		Gas					0	0	993	195	0	0	28	5
Lena-Anabar Basin AU (12000101) Aggregate *		Oil				1,919				1,507				41
		Gas								608				16
Lena-Anabar Updip AU (12000102)	0.800	Oil	0	0	524	56	0	0	338	44	0	0	9	1
		Gas					0	0	483	47	0	0	12	1
Sukhan-Motorchun Riphean Rift AU (12000103)	0.072	Oil	0	0	187	21	0	0	96	16	0	0	2	0
		Gas					0	0	465	39	0	0	11	1
Total undiscovered petroleum resources, Province 1200						1,996				2,261				60
LENA-VILYUI BASIN PROVINCE (1214) - Only one AU was assessed in this province														
Proterozoic-Paleozoic-Mesozoic Composite TPS (121401)														
Northern Priverkhoyansk Foredeep AU (12140101)	0.400	Oil	0	0	1,741	379	0	0	1,455	298	0	0	39	8
		Gas					0	0	4,341	1,044	0	0	117	28
Total undiscovered petroleum resources, assessed part of Province 1214						379				1,342				36
ZYRYANKA BASIN PROVINCE (1252)														
Paleozoic-Mesozoic Composite TPS (125201)														
Zyryanka Basin AU (12520101)	0.504	Oil	0	0	286	72	0	0	496	106	0	0	13	3
		Gas					0	942	7,746	2,176	0	22	209	58
Total undiscovered petroleum resources, Province 1252						72				2,282				61
Total undiscovered petroleum resources						8,031				105,850				2,832

[MMB, million barrels; BCF, billion cubic feet. Results shown are fully risked estimates. For gas fields, all liquids are included under the natural gas liquids (NGL) category. F95 denotes a 95-percent chance of at least the amount tabulated. Other fractiles are defined similarly. Fractiles are additive under the assumption of perfect positive correlation. TPS, total petroleum system; AU, assessment unit. Gray shading indicates not applicable]

*Aggregate means for the entire assessment unit equal the means times the scenario probability of each scenario.

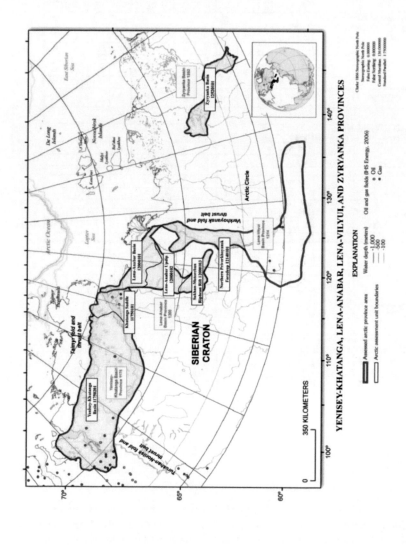

Figure 1. Map showing location of geologic provinces and assessment units along the northern and eastern margins of the Siberian craton north of the Arctic Circle.

In: Arctic Natural Resources
Editor: Brian D. Raney

ISBN: 978-1-60692-131-9
© 2009 Nova Science Publishers, Inc.

Chapter 5

ASSESSMENT OF UNDISCOVERED PETROLEUM RESOURCES OF THE LAPTEV SEA SHELF PROVINCE, RUSSIAN FEDERATION

United States Geological Survey

The Laptev Sea Shelf Province was assessed for undiscovered crude oil, natural gas, and natural gas liquids/condensates resources (collectively referred to as petroleum) as part of the U.S. Geological Survey's Circum-Arctic Oil and Gas Resource Appraisal. Using a geology-based methodology, the USGS estimates the mean undiscovered, conventional petroleum resources in the province to be approximately 9,300 million barrels of oil equivalent, including approximately 3,069 million barrels of crude oil, 32,252 billion cubic feet of natural gas, and 861 million barrels of natural gas liquids.

INTRODUCTION

In 2007, the U.S. Geological Survey (USGS) completed an assessment of potential undiscovered, technically recoverable (assuming the absence of sea ice) crude oil, natural gas, and natural gas liquids (collectively referred to as petroleum) resources in the Laptev Sea Shelf Province of the Russian Federation. As with other areas assessed in the USGS Circum-Arctic Oil and

Gas Resource Appraisal (CARA), this area shares important characteristics with many Arctic basins, including sparse data, significant petroleum-resource potential, geologic uncertainty, and technical barriers that impede exploration and development. As defined for CARA, the province includes an area of approximately 500,000 km^2, most of which underlies less than 500 m of water offshore of northern Russia between long. 110° and 150° E. and between lat. 70° and 80° N.

ASSESSMENT UNITS

The Laptev Sea Shelf Province contains a composite sedimentary basin, in which sediments were deformed by compression during Early Cretaceous time; later, in Paleogene and Neogene time, a superimposed rift/sag system developed in the area. The province was subdivided into three geologically distinctive assessment units based on structural style—the West Laptev Grabens, East Laptev Horsts, and Anisin-Novosibirsk Basins assessment units (AUs) (Figure 1). The West Laptev Grabens AU was evaluated using two different geological scenarios (table 1) because geologic models for petroleum occurrence considered for this AU are mutually exclusive. The differences between the two scenarios are so extreme that the populations of undiscovered accumulations cannot be statistically combined into a single distribution. The Anisin-Novosibirsk Basins AU was also assessed. The East Laptev Horsts AU, although defined, was not quantitatively assessed because of the extremely low assessment-unit probability for the existence of an undiscovered accumulation exceeding the defined minimum size of 50 million barrels of oil equivalent.

PETROLEUM SYSTEM ELEMENTS

Onshore field work and interpretation of geophysical data gathered from offshore areas by geologists from several countries and organizations indicate that two or more total petroleum systems might exist in the study area. Because of possible mixing of petroleum, the Jurassic-Cretaceous-Paleogene Composite Total Petroleum System (TPS) was identified for the West Laptev Grabens AU. Geologic scenarios evaluated for the assessment were based on the existence and distribution of source rocks of these ages. The Paleogene

TPS was identified for the Anisin-Novosibirsk Basins AU. The greatest geologic uncertainty for the assessment of both assessment units is with respect to the petroleum charge.

Analyses of natural gas collected from bottom sediments and near-bottom waters of the Laptev Sea Shelf indicate the presence of mature oil-prone marine source rocks, presumably of Paleogene age. Upper Jurassic (Volgian) organic-rich mudstone might also be an important petroleum source rock in the study area, as are synrift Lower Cretaceous and Paleogene carbonaceous and coaly rocks. Major synrift reservoir rocks are likely to be shelf and slope siliciclastic sediments deposited by deltas of the paleo- and present-day Lena River. Whether prerift reservoir rocks are present is uncertain. Traps for petroleum accumulation could include extensional structures and stratigraphic traps associated with shelf sediments.

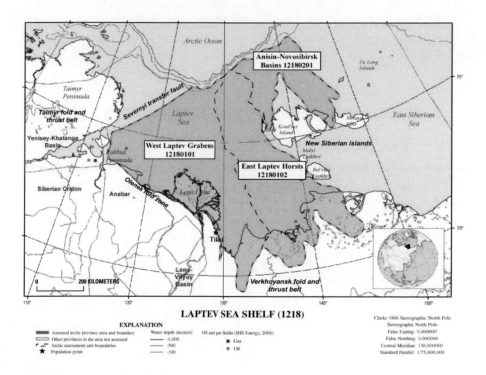

Figure 1. Map showing location of the Laptev Sea Shelf Province and assessment units.

RESOURCE SUMMARY

The U.S. Geological Survey assessed undiscovered conventional, technically recoverable petroleum (discovered reserves not included) resulting in the estimated mean volumes of a probability distribution of approximately 3,069 million barrels (419 million metric tons) of crude oil, 32,252 billion cubic feet (913 billion cubic meters) of natural gas, and 861 million barrels (117 million metric tons) of natural gas liquids (table 1). The greatest volume of undiscovered petroleum is estimated to be in the West Laptev Grabens AU.

REFERENCES

IHS Energy, 2006, [includes data current through December, 2005], International petroleum exploration and production database: IHS Energy; database available from IHS Energy, 15 Inverness Way East, Englewood, Colorado 80112 USA.

LAPTEV SEA SHELF PROVINCE ASSESSMENT TEAM

T.R. Klett (assessing geologist), Kenneth J. Bird, Philip J. Brown II, Ronald R. Charpentier, Donald L. Gautier, David W. Houseknecht, Thomas E. Moore, Janet K. Pitman, Richard W. Saltus, Christopher J. Schenk, and Marilyn E. Tennyson

ACKNOWLEGMENTS

Geographical Information System analysis was performed by Feliks Persits.

Table 1. Laptev Sea Shelf Province Assessment Results (Discovered Reserves not Included)

Total Petroleum Systems and Assessment Units	AU Prob-ability	Field Type	Oil (MMB)				Total Undiscovered Resources Gas (BCF)				NGL (MMB)			
			F95	F50	F5	Mean	F95	F50	F5	Mean	F95	F50	F5	Mean
LAPTEV SEA SHELF PROVINCE 1218) Jurassic-Cretaceous-Paleogene Composite TPS (121801)														
West Laptev Grabens AU (12100101) Scenario 1, 0.1% probability	1.00	Oil	3,344	12,790	38,691	15,861	4,221	17,699	62,602	23,545	111	470	1,694	633
		Gas					18,947	76,933	245,801	97,337	493	2,028	6,624	2,593
West Laptev Grabens AU (12100101) Scenario 2, 0.9% probability	0.49	Oil	0	0	4,251	1,127	0	0	6,587	1,660	0	0	177	45
		Gas					0	0	59,147	16,886	0	0	1,583	450
West Laptev Grabens AU (12100101) Aggregate*		Oil				2,600				3,049				104
		Gas								24,931				664
East Laptev Horsts AU (12100102)	0.03	Not quantitatively assessed												

Table 1. (Continued)

Total Petroleum Systems and Assessment Units	AU Prob-ability	Field Type	Oil (MMB)				Total Undiscovered Resources Gas (BCF)				NGL (MMB)			
			F95	F50	F5	Mean	F95	F50	F5	Mean	F95	F50	F5	Mean
Total undiscovered petroleum resources, TPS 121801						2,600				28,780				768
Paleogene TPS (121802)														
Anisin-Novosibirsk Basins AU (12100201)	0.43	Oil	0	0	1,837	469	0	0	2,901	693	0	0	79	19
		Gas					0	0	10,694	2,779	0	0	286	74
Total undiscovered petroleum resources, TPS 121802			0	0	1,837	469	0	0	13,595	3,472	0	0	365	93
Total undiscovered petroleum resources, Laptev Sea Shelf						3,069				32,252				861

[MMB, million barrels; BCF, billion cubic feet Results shown are fully risked estimates. For gas fields, all liquids are included under the natural gas liquids (NGL) category. F95 denotes a 95-percent chance of at least the amount tabulated. Other fractiles are defined similarly. Fractiles are additive under the assumption of perfect positive correlation. TPS,total petroleum system; AU, assessment unit Gray shading indicates not applicable]

* Aggregate means for the entire assessment unit equal the means times the scenario probability of each scenario

In: Arctic Natural Resources
Editor: Brian D. Raney

ISBN: 978-1-60692-131-9
© 2009 Nova Science Publishers, Inc.

Chapter 6

ASSESSMENT OF UNDISCOVERED OIL AND GAS RESOURCES OF THE EAST GREENLAND RIFT BASINS PROVINCE

United States Geological Survey

Northeast Greenland is the prototype for the U.S. Geological Survey's Circum-Arctic Oil and Gas Resource Appraisal. Using a geology-based methodology, the USGS estimates the mean undiscovered, conventional petroleum resources in the province to be approximately 31,400 MMBOE (million barrels of oil equivalent) of oil, gas, and natural gas liquids.

INTRODUCTION

In 2007 the U.S. Geological Survey (USGS) completed an assessment of the potential for undiscovered, technically recoverable (assuming the absence of sea ice) oil and gas resources in the East Greenland Rift Basins Province (fig. 1). Northeast Greenland has been selected as the prototype for the new U.S. Geological Survey Circum-Arctic Resource Appraisal (CARA) because the area shares important characteristics with many arctic basins, including sparse data, significant resource potential, great geological uncertainty, and significant technical barriers to exploration and development. This study, which supersedes a previous USGS assessment of the same area completed in 2000, was necessary because of new information made available through collaboration with the Geological Survey of Denmark and Greenland (GEUS), which significantly changes the geological understanding of the area.

As defined for CARA, the province includes an area of approximately 500,000 square kilometers, most of which underlies less than 500 meters of water offshore east of Greenland between 70° and 82° North.

ASSESSMENT UNITS

In collaboration with GEUS, the East Greenland Rift Basins Province was subdivided into seven geologically distinctive Assessment Units (AU), of which five were quantitatively assessed (Figure 1). These are: North Danmarkshavn Salt Basin, South Danmarkshavn Basin, Thetis Basin, Northeast Greenland Volcanic Province, and Liverpool Land Basin. Jameson Land Basin and the Jameson Land Basin Subvolcanic Extension were defined as AUs but were not quantitatively assessed.

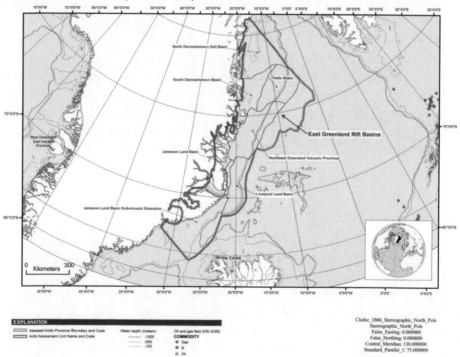

Figure 1. East Greenland Rift Basins.

PETROLEUM SYSTEM ELEMENTS

Onshore studies by GEUS and other organizations suggest that at least four stratigraphic intervals may contain potentially good source rocks for liquid petroleum. On the basis of considerations of the geological history of related areas in western Norway and burial history modeling, Upper Jurassic strata are believed to contain particularly promising petroleum source rocks. Possible trapping mechanisms are expected to vary widely across the province. Potential traps in the North Danmarkshavn Salt Basin AU are dominated by structures formed through salt tectonics; those in the Southern Danmarkshavn Basin and the Northeast Greenland Volcanic Province probably are characterized by extensional structures and by stratigraphic traps in submarine fan complexes. Prospective inversion structures of Tertiary age are present along the western margin of South Danmarkshavn Basin AU, and the large horst block structures, which separate the Danmarkshavn and Thetis Basins, may provide numerous opportunities for traps in fault blocks, along a major unconformity and in various facies-related permeability barriers. Possible reservoirs are considered most likely within shallow marine to nonmarine sandstones of Middle Jurassic age, in Upper Jurassic synrift deposits, in Cretaceous sandstones in submarine fan complexes, within progradational sequences of Paleogene age, and in Upper Carboniferous to Lower Permian warm-water carbonate sequences, especially in northern Danmarkshavn Basin. Marine shales are expected to provide the main sealing lithologies in most AUs.

RESOURCE SUMMARY

Most of the undiscovered oil, gas, and natural gas liquids is likely in the offshore parts of the province and is inferred to belong to an Upper Jurassic Composite Total Petroleum System. The resource estimates for the East Greenland Rift Basins Province and for the various AUs are tabulated in table 1. The USGS estimates that the East Greenland Rift Basins Province contains approximately (mean) 31,400 MMBOE of oil, natural gas, and natural gas liquids.Of the five assessed AUs, North Danmarkshavn Salt Basin and the South Danmarkshavn Basin are estimated to contain the most of the undiscovered petroleum resources.

Table 1. East Greenland and Rift Province Assessment Results

Total Petroleum Systems (TPS) and Assessment Units (AU)	AU Probability	Field Type	Total Undiscovered Resources											
			Oil (MMBO)				Gas (BCFG)				NGL (MMBNGL)			
			F95	F50	F5	Mean	F95	F50	F5	Mean	F95	F50	F5	Mean
North Danmarkshavn Salt Basin AU	0.65	Oil	0	1,989	11,793	3,274	0	3,827	26,779	7,255	0	264	2,123	570
		Gas					0	23,820	107,409	32,756	0	2,284	10,730	3,237
South Danmarkshavn Basin AU	0.72	Oil	0	3,228	13,996	4,384	0	6,325	32,081	9,709	0	449	2,603	761
		Gas					0	19,344	83,621	26,251	0	1,844	8,362	2,598
Northeast Greenland Volcanic Province AU	0.26	Oil	0	0	2,757	497	0	0	6,212	1,105	0	0	492	87
		Gas					0	0	16,551	3,003	0	0	1,651	297
Thetis Basin AU	0.49	Oil	0	0	2,095	537	0	0	4,908	1,184	0	0	397	93
		Gas					0	0	12,489	3,206	0	0	1,251	317
Liverpool Land Basin AU	0.29	Oil	0	0	1,122	209	0	0	2,528	464	0	0	200	37
		Gas					0	0	6,740	1,255	0	0	672	124
Jameson Land Basin AU	0.07	Oil	Not quantitatively assessed											
		Gas												
Jameson Land Basin Subvolcanic Extension AU	0.04	Oil	Not quantitatively assessed											
		Gas												
Total Conventional Resources						8,901				86,179				8,121

[MMBO, million barrerls of oil, BCFG, billion cubic feet of gas, MMBNGL, millon barrels of natural gas liquids. Results are fully risked estimates. For gas accumulators, all liquids are included as NGL (natural gas liquids). F95 represents a 95-percent chance at least the amount tabulated; other fractiles are defined similarly. Fractiles are additive under the assumption of perfect positive correlation. TPS, total petroleum system AU, assessment unit. Gray shading indicates not applicable.]

Wegener Halvø (seen from southeast to the northwest): Devonian below unconformity, Permian carbonate build-ups overlain by Ravnefjeld formation source rock and Wordie Creek formation mudstones.Photograph by Stefan Piasecki (GEUS).

East Greenland Rift Basins Province Assessment Team

Donald L. Gautier, Kenneth J. Bird, Ronald R. Charpentier, David Houseknecht, Timothy R. Klett, Christopher J. Schenk, Marilyn E. Tennyson

ACKNOWLEDGMENT

While the resource estimates reported here are the product and responsibility of the U.S. Geological Survey, the geological analysis of northeastern Greenland used for this study was completed in collaboration with GEUS, the Geological Survey of Denmark and Greenland.

Katedralen/Ugleelv in Jameson Land: Jurassic succession with Sortehat formation,Pelion formation (reservoir sandstone), Fossilbjerg formation, and Hareelv formation(source rock). Photograph by Stefan Piasecki (GEUS).

In: Arctic Natural Resources
Editor: Brian D. Raney

ISBN: 978-1-60692-131-9
© 2009 Nova Science Publishers, Inc.

Chapter 7

ASSESSMENT OF UNDISCOVERED OIL AND GAS RESOURCES OF THE WEST GREENLAND—EAST CANADA PROVINCE, 2008

United States Geological Survey

Using a geology-based assessment methodology, the U.S. Geological Survey estimated a mean of 7.3 billion barrels of oil and a mean of 52 trillion cubic feet of undiscovered natural gas in the West Greenland—East Canada Province north of the Arctic Circle.

INTRODUCTION

The U.S. Geological Survey (USGS) recently assessed the undiscovered oil and gas potential of the West Greenland—East Canada Province as part of the USGS Circum-Arctic Oil and Gas Resource Appraisal effort. The West Greenland—East Canada Province is essentially the offshore area between west Greenland and east Canada and includes Baffin Bay, Davis Strait, Lancaster Sound, and Nares Strait west of and including Kane Basin (Figure 1). The tectonic evolution of the West Greenland—East Canada Province led to the formation of several major structural domains that are the geologic basis for the five assessment units (AU) defined in this study (Figure 1). The five

AUs encompass the entire province Each AU was assessed in its entirety for undiscovered, technically recoverable (assuming absence of sea ice) oil and gas resources, but the assessment results reported here are only for those portions of each AU that are north of the Arctic Circle, as that latitude defines the area of the Circum-Arctic oil and gas assessment.

GEOLOGIC DEFINITION OF ASSESSMENT UNITS

The tectonic evolution of the West Greenland—East Canada province was complex and included (1) at least two phases of Cretaceous rifting and thermal subsidence between west Greenland and Canada; (2) counterclockwise rotation of Greenland driven largely by adjacent plate movements and the thermal effects of mantle plumes; (3) the development of the Ungava transform fault zone concomitant with the opening of Baffin Bay basin and the Labrador Sea; and (4) compression in the northern part of the province (Eurekan Orogeny) as Greenland rotated and collided with Canada in the Paleogene (Harrison and others, 1999; Funck and others, 2007). The AUs reflect this geologic history. The Eurekan Structures AU (AU-1, Figure 1) is characterized by inverted structures developed in the northern part of the province during the Eurekan Orogeny. The North-west Greenland Rifted Margin AU (AU-2, Figure 1) and the North-east Canada Rifted Margin AU (AU-3, Figure 1) encompass the rifted, conjugate continental margins. The Baffin Bay Basin AU (AU-4, Figure 1) reflects the oceanic(?) part of Baffin Bay where there is greater than 8 km of sediment. The Greater Ungava Fault Zone AU (AU-5, Figure 1) includes strike-slip structures along a broad zone of the Ungava transform fault.

The USGS defined a Mesozoic-Cenozoic Composite Total Petroleum System (TPS) in the West Greenland–East Canada Province; the five AUs are included within this TPS. Several petroleum source rocks are postulated to be present, including possible source rocks within Ordovician, Lower and Upper Cretaceous, and Paleogene stratigraphic intervals (Bojesen-Koefoed and others, 1999, 2004).

RESOURCE SUMMARY

The USGS assessed undiscovered technically recoverable conventional oil and gas resources in the five AUs within the Mesozoic- Cenozoic TPS, but the resource estimates reported here are only for those portions of the AUs that are north of the Arctic Circle (table 1). For conventional resources in the West Greenland-East Canada Province, the estimated means were 7,275 million barrels of oil (MMBO), 51,816 billion cubic feet of natural gas (BCFG), and 1,152 million barrels of natural-gas liquids (MMBNGL). The assessment indicates that about half of undiscovered oil and gas resources in the province are estimated to be in the rifted margin AUs (table 1).

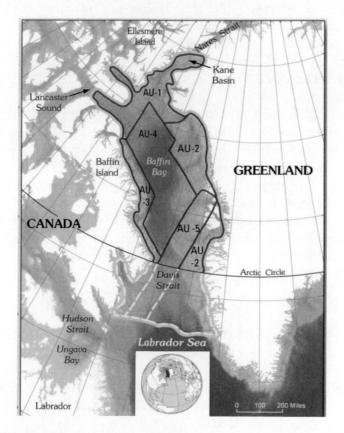

Figure 1. The West Greenland–East Canada Province (tan line) contains Baffin Bay, Davis Strait, Lancaster Sound, and Nares Strait west of and including Kane Basin. Five assessment units (red lines) were defined in this study: AU-1, Eurekan Structures AU; AU-2, Northwest Greenland Rifted Margin AU; AU-3, Northeast Canada Rifted

Margin AU; AU-4, Baffin Bay Basin AU; AU-5, Greater Ungava Fault Zone AU. Dashed yellow lines represent portions of those AUs that extend south of the Arctic Circle.

REFERENCES

Bojesen-Koefoed, J. A., Christiansen, F. G., Nytoft, H. P. & Pedersen, A. K. (1999). Oil seepage onshore West Greenland- Evidence of multiple source rocks and oil mixing, *in* Fleet, A.J., and Boldy, S.A.R., eds., Petroleum geology of northwest Europe. Proceedings of the 5th Conference: Geological Society of London, p. 305-314.

Bojesen-Koefoed, J. A., Nytoft, H. P. & Christiansen, F. G. (2004). Age of oils in West Greenland-Was there a Mesozoic seaway between Greenland and Canada?: Geological Survey of Denmark and Greenland Bulletin, v. 4, p. 49-52.

Funck, T., Jackson, H. R., Louden, K. E. & Klingelhofer, F. (2007). Seismic study of the transform-rifted margin in Davis Strait between Baffin Island (Canada) and Greenland-What happens when a plume meets a transform: Journal of Geophysical Research, v. 112, B04402, 22 p.

Harrison, J. C., Mayr, U., McNeil, D. H., Sweet, A. R., McIntyre, D. J., Eberle, J. J., Harington, C. R., Chalmers, J. A., Dam, G. & Nohr-Hansen, H.. (1999). Correlation of Cenozoic sequences of the Canadian Arctic region and Greenland- Implications for the tectonic history of northern North America: Canadian Petroleum Geology Bulletin, v. 47, no. 3, p. 223-254.

WEST GREENLAND-EAST CANADA PROVINCE ASSESSMENT TEAM

Christopher J. Schenk, Kenneth J. Bird, Philip J. Brown II, Ronald R. Charpentier, Donald L. Gautier, David W. Houseknecht, Timothy R. Klett, Mark J. Pawlewicz, Anjana Shah, and Marilyn E. Tennyson.

Table 1. West Greenland-East Canada Province Assessment Results

Total Petroleum Systems (TPS) and Assessment Units (AU)	AU Proba-bility	Field Type	Total Undiscovered Resources											
			Oil (MMBO)				Gas (BCFG)				NGL (MMBNGL)			
			F95	F50	F5	Mean	F95	F50	F5	Mean	F95	F50	F5	Mean
Mesozoic-Cenozoic Composite TPS														
Eurekan Structures AU	0.25	Oil	0	0	6,626	1,133	0	0	10,490	1,784	0	0	285	48
		Gas					0	0	39,428	6,806	0	0	1,055	181
Northwest Greenland Rifted Margin AU	0.50	Oil	0	260	10,900	2,746	0	157	10,488	2,547	0	4	237	57
		Gas					0	1,090	61,086	15,251	0	25	1,386	339
Northeast Canada Rifted Margin AU	0.50	Oil	0	0	3,470	850	0	0	3,318	787	0	0	76	18
		Gas					0	0	17,577	4,374	0	0	418	97
Baffin Bay Basin AU	0.28	Oil	0	0	8,470	1,555	0	0	16,128	2,934	0	0	244	44
		Gas					0	0	50,598	9,338	0	0	1,126	206
Greater Ungava Fault Zone AU	0.30	Oil	0	0	5,037	991	0	0	11,105	2,143	0	0	195	38
		Gas					0	0	29,950	5,852	0	0	635	124
Total Conventional Resources						**7,275**				**51,816**				**1,152**

[MMBO, million barrels of oil. BCFG, billion cubic feet of gas. MMBNGL, million barrels of natural gas liquids. Results shown are fully risked estimates. For gas accumulations, all liquids are included as NGL (natural gas liquids). Undiscovered gas resources are the sum of nonassociated and associated gas. F95 represents a 95 percent chance of at least the amount tabulated; other fractiles are defined similarly. AU probability is the chance of at least one accumulation of minimum size within the AU. TPS, total petroleum system; AU, assessment unit. Gray shading indicates not applicable]

CHAPTER SOURCES

The following chapters have been previously published:

Chapter 1- This is an edited, reformatted and augmented version of a Congressional Research Service Report for Congress, Report RL32838 dated April 9, 2007.

Chapter 2 - This is an edited, reformatted and augmented version of a Congressional Research Service Report for Congress, Report RS22143 dated February 1, 2006.

Chapter 3 - This is an edited, reformatted and augmented version of a United States Geological Survey, Report 2008-1193.

Chapter 4 - This is an edited, reformatted and augmented version of a United States Geological Survey, Report 2008-3020.

Chapter 5 - This is an edited, reformatted and augmented version of a United States Geological Survey, Report 2007-3096.

Chapter 6 - This is an edited, reformatted and augmented version of a United States Geological Survey, Report 2007-3077.

Chapter 7 - This is an edited, reformatted and augmented version of a United States Geological Survey, Report 2008-3014.

INDEX

M

N

O

P